I0435442

ISBN – 13: 978-153080969807

ISBN – 10: 153-0969808

This book printed in the United States of America

JM Publishing Plus

# Our

# Christian

# Republic

George R. Melcher

# Contents

5

# Introduction

I have written this small book as a snapshot of the history of our republic, drawn some seventy years previous to its triumphant conclusion in 1778. Upon examination concerning the fortitude and resilience of the people who began building a nation from thirteen sovereign colonies. This after winning an unpopular war with a strong nation of substantial military power and indeed the most powerful empire in the world.

After the war these men worked out a Constitution of magnificent significance, while promising the utmost assurance of God given unalienable rights, with a truly functional freedom, one the world had never before realized.

Therefore, one would expect We the People to protect the inheritance given us from God and the sacrifice of the people who established our republic. In its place today we find more readily an attitude of me first from the people and a government rearranging our Constitution or ignoring it completely, this occurring through all three branches of government.

This written sketch is my method to present the diminutive years following the God inspired, man crafted, realizing a new self-possessed new design for government. As a result the purpose was intended, so government of the sovereign states would establish their own rules, laws and self-control.

There were a few agreed upon rules put in place for the national government to fulfill, hence appropriately controlled by citizens chosen from the sovereign states. Thus the national government was created, composed of people elected from and of whose power only existed, and derived from the consent of those governed, moreover this idea was so innovative, unexperienced plus untested leaving most citizens with a freedom never before established or entrusted for their undertaking. This new liberty came while many folks were moving west as far as the Mississippi river and some beyond, building new areas, exploratory, adventurous yet dangerous, thus expanding the progress for its fast growing population. As many people in the south carried on farming great cotton and tobacco plantations, those in the north further grew and improved the industrial age.

All the while fewer citizens engaged themselves or cultivated time for their own government, therefore the Central Government proceeded to transform and influence the power awaiting them, eager to exploit the opportunity over those with a lesser amount of awareness and of the growing central government with its desire to arrest power from the individual sovereign states. Thus by 1850 there were 30 states with sixty Senators two hundred thirty three House members. Their altered power through continued proliferation of state sovereignty, this in earnest until this very day. Let's not forget the reconstruction era just prior to the turn of the century, was a disgraceful episode in our history.

After our humbled republic went through a great depression, World War 11, then a presidential assassination, losing the war on poverty and Viet Nam, thus creating these events literally assured our Republic the pathway to socialism.

This now demands that we take a serious look at the situation we are facing today, with the most disgusting and repelling liar ever to sit in the oval office. A man who chose to claim being Negro, rather than the Mulatto person he was born, again a lie which began and became his practice of being notoriously deceiving our people

Then who became his closest ally, a socialist, Muslim woman named Valerie Jarrett. Why then should we be at all astonished concerning this offensive person, when her activities exposed her objectives and is recognized as Obama's utmost confidant, remaining to this day, seeking ways to create chaos for our Republic.

Inside you will find a well-defined explanation of facts and my views on these issues, plus an analysis of these facts and a prospect, perhaps better yet, a proposal for the restoration of our republic's orginal Christian goals.

The objective and desire for this quite small-scaled book, was written for the reader to discover various examples, of our national government's acquisition of power, acquired and assimilated adversely. Hopefully these thoughts will have a significant effect upon the reader and as a result, will give reason for greater participation and interest in our republic.

**Part One**

**The antithesis of our Republic's initial ideals, which led to its demise.**

This narrative is intended to convey the essence of my thoughts regarding our republic, all within this small book, actually a trilogy. You will find there are but three distinct parts to this dissertation spanning roughly 235 years, plus some men's malfeasant ambitions to weaken and/or change our Constitution, doing so devoid of the people's choice deciding its central and indispensable qualifications. Doing this rather than selecting the amendment procedure, our Constitution need not be convoluted or weakened by those persons choosing to do so, particularly for their own wanting. While conversion, if conditions are required, an honest and impartial course has been established.

Secondly, an illustration of just how our current, corrupt government, at its highest level has deprived or should I say robbed, the people of their autonomy. All the while devastating the core of our nation the middle class, the working people, the only stable portion of our republic. I have chosen the United States Supreme Court as a convincing example, revealing just how significantly politics has fallen to money, power and corruption.

Then thirdly I ask, where is our verve, our enthusiasm now? Why are we not once again conducting ourselves as our fathers, developing our society, seeking the help of God? I believe there's an immense necessity for putting an end to socialism, overcoming the present government we have and absolutely punish those who have deliberately scorned God, disparaged Christianity, committing crimes against our Republic and its people.

I believe we are at the cross roads, the tipping point for the survival of our republic, let me once again quote the words of patriot Patrick Henry, "*Gentlemen may cry peace, peace, but there is no peace. The war is actually begun! The next gale that sweeps the*

11

*north will bring to our ears the clash of resounding arms! Our brethren are already in the field. I know not what course others may take; but as for me, give me liberty, or give me death!"*

These words may sound stark or abrasive, but it appears to me we have arrived at that position, the sound of clashing arms are nearing us and we have men all over the middle-east, I ask, then what course shall we take? It seems a catalogue of choices are not available, a decision must be made soon, waiting till after the 2016 election is not a choice, nor will the appearance of action, only the dedication for reaching a winning strategy need be grasped, our goal has been scheduled for us.

We the People, must crave the responsibility by accepting the power granted in the Constitution, therefore returning control of government to the states, above all seeking God's wisdom, provisions and blessings as He is on our side, failure will only come if we forsake Him and neglect our compulsory need of repentance, individually and collectively.

The intent of this book though conceivably undersized in volume, nevertheless written to reach the citizens of our once great republic, who in my opinion are gullible or generally unaware of why or how our union was formed through exercising Christian concepts. Without question, we have unequivocally created the most brilliantly established government administrated by man, however originated and initiated by God, completed by wise men giving their lives, fortunes and their sacred honor.

While time or place is not paramount to reference the actual events, however the early 1700 hundreds is a major and significant place to begin these painstaking introspective words. Thus this remarkable experiment called independence with personal liberty and owing to those liberties given by God, inaugurated initiatives and attitudes born of people with different objectives. All coming together from the thirteen colonies, each were quite determined this would materialize for people governing people, by those chosen from the people.

The foremost consideration was sovereignty for each colony and each person therein and not controlled from far off England. I feel at this juncture ii all good conscience one needs suggest its Washington D. C. today as being far off, truly far off.

Now of course not all colonist felt that desire and by necessity were of the opinion, protection from an invasion of France or Spain was a priority. Therefore a confrontation between the two ideologies ensued for some seventy years, including many choosing a return to England. Queen Anne was the creature of several wars which England was either ceded by France or by an outright takeover, as was Nova Scotia. However the story of those 13 colonies (New Hampshire, Massachusetts, Connecticut, Rhode Island, New York, New Jersey, Pennsylvania, Delaware, Maryland, Virginia, North and South Carolina and Georgia) were not an assemblage of colonies brought together by England, rather at different times and by diverse political interest. The following are for the most part and thus best known as proprietary colonies, Pennsylvania, Delaware, New York, New Jersey, and Maryland furthermore, they were governed much as royal colonies. While perhaps New Hampshire, Virginia, North Carolina, South Carolina and Georgia, were provincial, thus described as royal colonies.

While Massachusetts, Rhode Island, and Connecticut were charter colonies, though conceivably as an alternative the New England, Middle and the southern, which leaves us to another confusion as which colony fit into their political expressions.

Nevertheless, Queen Anne's era other than the so called Queen's War, the citizens were for the most part, having the slightest interest in any separation from England, their mother land.

The next period of control for the colonies came from King George the First, who held a little tighter jurisdiction over them, this brought some concern to a number of particular political persons, however his rule ended 1727, while there was judiciousness in general, though some specific anxieties prevailed. When King George the Second began rule in 1727 through 1760 disturbing disquiet existed and many colonist began to feel bitter about his attitude and his expended exploitations, while he was governing the colonies.

Colonial era diplomacy focused on two issues: the European balance of power and the colonists' appropriation of land from the Native Americans. Rivalry in Europe, between the French and British in particular, often influenced the course of events in their North American colonies.

An effort increased by both the British and the French in order for their political and economic power to strengthen, the British and French vied to acquire the larger share of the available land and control over the new trading opportunities the colonies presented. For this period of time, the European colonial governments tried to find ways to coexist with the original inhabitants, often by building alliances with certain tribes while triggering alienation with others. Sometimes, as in the case of the French and Indian War which in Europe was referred to as the (Seven Year War), European balance of power and politics, resulted in conflict in the colonies. As wars in Europe became more heated, fighting broke out between the French and the British in the American colonies. Both sides called upon Native American allies to assist them, exacerbating tensions between the tribes. Ultimately, the British Government found it necessary to pour additional troops and resources into protecting its possessions in the Americas and taxed their colonists to pay for it. These taxes eventually developed into a rallying cry for the colonial movement of independence.

The Albany Plan of Union, was a plan to place the British North American colonies under a more centralized government. On July 10, 1754, representatives from seven of the British North American colonies adopted the plan. Although never carried out, the Albany Plan was the first important proposal conceived of the colonies as a collective whole united under one government.   At the _Albany Congress_ of 1754, proposed by Benjamin Franklin for the colonies, therefore this plan became united by a Grand Council administering a common policy for defense, expansion, and Indian affairs. While the plan was thwarted by colonial legislatures and King George II, it was an early indication that the British colonies were headed towards unification and a discreet exchange concerning a separation from Great Britain.

Prior to the notion of the suggestion for "Albany Congress", a number of intellectuals and government officials had articulated and published several tentative plans for centralizing the colonial governments. Imperial officials saw the advantages of bringing the colonies under closer authority and supervision, while colonists saw it as the need to organize and defend common interests. One figure of emerging prominence among this group of intellectuals was Pennsylvanian Benjamin Franklin. As earlier, Franklin had written to friends and colleagues proposing a plan of "voluntary union for the colonies". The Pennsylvania government appointed Franklin as a commissioner to the Congress and on his journey, Franklin wrote to several New York commissioners outlining brief hints towards a scheme for uniting the Northern Colonies thru measures enacted by the British Parliament.

The progression of events finally led to organization for further and stronger agendas, guided by their own religious faith, rather than that of Great Britain's Anglican Church.

It had long been understood that the prime motive for the founding of the New England colonies was religious freedom. Certainly what those early colonists wanted was the freedom to worship God as they deemed appropriate. Much of the religious disaffection that found its way across the Atlantic Ocean, stemmed from disagreements within the Anglican Church, as this was the title for the Church of England. Those who sought to reform Anglican religious practices to "purify" the church became known as Puritans. They argued that the Church of England was following religious practices that too closely resembled Catholicism both in structure and ceremony. The Anglican clergy was organized along Episcopalian lines, with a hierarchy of bishops and archbishops. Puritans called for a Congregationalist structure in which each individual church would be largely self-governing. This concept by and large was adopted and indicated the beginning of their revolt against Great Britain.

The subject of their religious faith became the main discontent and ultimate issue leading to the revolt aimed at their separation from European control, primarily England. The Boston Tea Party in Dec. 1773 was a significant event in the growth of the American Revolution. The English Parliament responded in 1774 with the Coercive Acts, or as many seen it as the Intolerable Acts, which among other provisions, ended local self-government in Massachusetts closing Boston's commerce. Other colonists up and down the Thirteen Colonies responded in turn, the Coercive Acts with added acts of protest, and led to the convening of the First Continental Congress, which petitioned the British Monarch for repeal of the acts, this really organized the colonial resistance to British control of their political and religious lives. In short the crisis escalated, and the American Revolutionary War began straightforward near Boston in 1775.

The next act by the colonists was a total rebellion, so declared by signing the Declaration of Independence, adopted by the Continental Congress of the thirteen colonies on the 4ᵗʰ day of July 1776. As one could expect war broke out and victory would bring about freedom from England and represent to all of Europe a self-governing union of soveriegn states, a newfound republic. Furthermore, these sovereign states would create a national Constitution with limited and enumerated powers, thus bringing together these sovereign states into a unification of efforts. Thereby establishing a national government assembled, occupied with full control by the people and of the people's legislators, of these sovereign states.

Hence a republic of soveriegn states, under God who had granted them freedom , therefore bestowing upon them certain unalienable rights, among them Life, Liberty and the pursuit of happiness and to secure these rights, governments are instituted among men, deriving their just powers from the consent of the governed. Words and principles from the Declaration of Independence.

This statement given at the Constitutional Convention by George Washington *"If, to please the people, yet we ourselves disapprove, how can we, afterwards defend our work? Let us raise a standard to which the wise and honest men can repair. This event is in the hand of God."* It seems quite obvious this new republic was formed and sustained by God and was shaped in Christianity through its laws and principles. Regardless of the many approaches of worshiping God, it was most certainly Christianity at the core of all practices of worship and the foundation of our united soveriegn states.

16

Today as you walk up the steps to the Capitol Building which houses the Supreme Court you can see near the top of the building a row of the world's great law givers and each one is facing one in the middle who is facing forward with a full frontal view it is Moses with the Ten Commandments!

James Madison, the fourth president, known as "The Father of Our Constitution" made the following statement *"We have staked the whole of all our political institutions upon the capacity of mankind for self-government, upon the capacity of each and all of us to govern ourselves, to control ourselves, to sustain ourselves according to the Ten Commandments of God."*

Patrick Henry, that patriot and Founding Father of our country said, *"It cannot be emphasized too strongly or too often that this great nation was founded not by religionists but by Christians...not on religions but on the Gospel of Jesus Christ".*

Without any reservation or doubt this is a Christian nation, as in our pledge of allegiance, "one nation under God" still remains in most of our schools. While that event along with the Ten Commandments have been removed from some courts, along with other public places to appease particular groups who fail to understand our Christian heritage. Nevertheless, still unopposed by many so called Christians.

I find it astounding, while less than a mere seventy five years, We the People succumb to a man (Lincoln) so inflicted with tyranical and deceptive schemes, one is astonished he had been elected to the presidency. Hence leading them/us to chaos, after which the people followed like sheep down a path of obvious lies. This man suspended the Writ of Habeas Corpus and jailed all who contradicted or dissented against him, including judges. Shutdown the press if they felt obligated by their awareness to print conflicting thoughts and compete against his ideology.

Yet not a whimper was heard from Christians, they were silent, the silence became defining and old Abe marched on, leaving 650,000 dead behind. Rather the landmark federal legislation which prohibited discrimination on the basis of race, color, religion, sex and national origin never arrived upon the scene until The Civil Rights Act of 1964. This granted equal access to employment, schools and public spaces.

Accordingly, Lincoln remained without strategy for the emancipation of the Negro

17

slaves, after they had gained their freedom. In the same fashion, he had failed to form any concepts or proposals for operational viewpoints to solve this conundrum. All these free persons he had positioned into a society being quite unprepared for such a situation. I ask where would they live, work or worship, this problem only grew more corrupt and ruthless as time marched on and remained in disarray, turmoil and disorder. It seemed again that Christians were absent from society as the misery grew and grew until the fore mention Civil Rights Act. Once more, some fifty years later indications shows but a negligible improvement between White and Black personal relationships. While the sixties were a phenomena to many, I find the occurrences of diverse issues and mean while the people chose poor leaders, unable to properly guide us through these turbulent times. Acts such as these regarding governmental action or inaction perhaps confusing issues remind you of this today.

Then along came Teddy Roosevelt a real autocratic, a dictatorial character to whom the Congress meant little, only persons in the way for a menus of his designs. The old Rough Rider built the Panama Canal Zone however the cost to construct the Panama Canal was $375 million, including $10 million paid to Panama plus $40 million paid to the French Canal Company for the rights to build the canal. Moreover, the bodies beyond that of 22,000 men, thus irritating the Columbian government.

We find a progressive man in President Wilson, whose problem was not dealing with the Constitution, as he felt he could cope with and manage that difficulty. Rather, he stated "it's that pesky Declaration of Independence".

Franklin D. Roosevelt arrived on the scene in the early days of the depression, and generated a plight appallingly more injurious, to the people and the soveriegn states. This man instigated a war with Japan and in so doing added Germany and Italy, which on the whole certainly achieved one tricky obstruction, the depression our republic was mired. He had accomplished this at the cost of thousands and thousands of American lives. Roosevelt joined the trio of Winston Churchill, Charles De Gaulle and Josef Stalin to put together quite a quartet in order to defeat Adolf Hitler and his infamous group.

18

While in office, to arrive at his desired agendas, he went so far as trying to add four judges to the U.S. Supreme Court. Though knowing he was the only man to be elected four terms as president, certainly having the justification to state that he was popular with the people, regardless of his political activities.

He had accomplished this at the cost of thousands and thousands American lives. Roosevelt joined the trio of Winston Churchill, Charles De Gaulle and Josef Stalin to put together quite a quartet in order to defeat Adolf Hitler and his infamous group.

Moving on to John F Kennedy a young man who served in the navy on a PT Boat and received two medals for his heroism. As president it was his "Civil Rights" Act which we spoke of earlier and for a time quieted the issue of race relations. In the sphere of national relationships, his action for a time decreased tensions with Cuba. Sometime later the flawed action called the Bay of Pigs was a complete and utter failure.

While we were given a slogan "the war on poverty", instead of a war on poverty it was a war in Viet Nam. This war which we failed to win, cost immeasurably in lives and treasure. Once again We the People, chose a man with considerable political power, but scarcely any character, in fact little more than a loud mouth from Texas, but created a law in the tax code which prevented Christians from speaking out against the government, nor support for any one candidate or another. This law would prevent churches if they spoke out, to claim a tax exempt status. This was accepted by Christians without a word of rightist or moral indignation, to this day. We find money the leading light here of all places, Christian Churches.

Then we were exposed to King Richard, tricky dickey Nixon, who finally ended our involvement in Viet Nam, surrendering after a tremendous loss of American life, not considering the Asians. However the king capitulated, removing himself from office in the face of impeachment, after this he swore "I'm no crook", nevertheless he was and the king was gone.

We the people relinquished their God given rights, whining to each other as to their plight, in between was a man who professed being a Christian, one Jimmy Carter. Then next to arrive in contrast to the past incompetent and unscrupulous persons,

19

came a man named Reagan. This ex-governer from California was a relaxed man, who brought some recovery from the previous adverse personalities. The few new ideas he brought with him as president, helped to improve our economy and an understanding of the Russian leaders. Thus this bold statement, Mr. Gorbachev, tear down this wall, meaning the Berlin wall which had become a symbol of communist oppression, built in 1961.

Now we couple his actions with a Constitutional question over the infusion of the "Iran -contra" and corrupt clandestine action, never approved by the United States Congress. Despite denials from the president, Vice President George Bush, and other Reagan officials that the CIA had nothing to do with the flights to Nicaragua. were used to covertly fund the Contra war in Nicaragua. Persistent investigations by journalists and Congress began to unravel the so-called Iran-Contra scandal. The scandal involved the secret sale of U.S. weapons to Iran (which was supposed to help in the release of U.S. hostages in the Middle East). It began in 1985, when the administration supplied weapons to Iran. This in his desire for securing the release of American hostages held by Hezbollah terrorists. So much for President Reagan and his tenure.

Then there was President George H. Bush and the "read my lips" quote, this with his promise for no new taxes, of course that promise never materialized. Let's not forget the thousand points of light statement, I have only to speculate as to what that implied.

Then there's Billy Boy Clinton a woman hunter, a schoolboy obsesed with sex. Sometime later twisting and meandering his way to the Presidency, justifiably suited for the job as there were more women to exploit. To the extreme he had swarmed too hard, too long, thus somewhat as expected, near the finish he befittingly faltered and as a result was impeached by the House of Representatives for lying under oath. This man being married to Hillary a person fascinated with politics while crafting Billy's run for the Presidency and the presumption she would rise to the presidency. In my opinion, Hillary's more than 35 years in politics, generated no creditable decisions or commendable solutions or achievements.

Promptly we found another immature fellow, elected him as president who soon claimed to be a warrior. When landing on the aircraft carrier, Abraham Lincoln on which a banner read "Mission Accomplished" therefore the president went on to state that this was the end to major combat operations in Iraq. Bush's assertion soon turned to bite him and quickly developed into controversy. Then almost immediately guerrilla warfare in Iraq increased during the Iraqi insurgency. The vast majority of casualties, both military and civilian, occurred after his speech.

After glimpsing into a few but various activities regarding a number of our recent past presidents, we will close with the examination of Barack Obama, a person so occupied of himself it becomes difficult to articulate between the two, the many facades in his warped personality. I am astonished how one person could stand in front of the American people, willfully and wantonly lie, so numerous times it's impossible to register.

Then Obama gave away programs for persons unwilling to work has obviously help hinder any improvement in our economy. His attack on Christianity is blatant and manifested in his law suits with Christian organizations. Furthermore, his willingness to accept influence from Muslim Clerics and is unwilling to give a negative response to Islam extremist, while Valerie Jarrett, chief advisor to Obama, some say the most powerful person in the White House, even more so than Obama.

ISNA was found to be a co-conspirator in the *Holy Land Foundation* case, guilty of funneling millions of dollars to Hamas. The head of ISNA, Mohamed Magid, was fêted at the White House as recently as last August, seated next to Obama at the Iftar, (Legions of Aa'une)" dinner, a place normally reserved for heads of state. Think about this for a moment, the head of an organization found guilty of funneling money to terrorists sitting next to the President of the United States. The statement by Mayor

21

Giuliani he believed Obama didn't love America, nor you and I. Furthermore, I would add, has a Muslim any love for Christianity, this idea presented, permits no possibilities. .

Since its ultimatum persist, it is incumbent upon us for the indispensable return to the simple principles of our constitution. I stand baffled at the failure of Congress to act upon the impeachment of President Obama, a man who has commited so many deliberate lies and failed to preserve, protect and defend our Constitution. In fact just the opposite, he actually trashed wretchedly and shredded instead of supporting. In my opinion his desire is to abolish the Constitution plus any and all laws he deemed unnecessary or created laws as he wished. This exists in my mind as he is an evil man, not worthy in any way to be trusted with any role in anyway within all our government. Moreover it's sad we are exposed to his presence whatsoever, in any case I question, WHY has this matter progressed without impeachment?

President Obama, a man who has commited so many deliberate lies and failed to preserve, protect and defend our Constitution. In fact just the opposite, he actually trashed wretchedly and shredded instead of supporting. In my opinion his desire is to abolish the Constitution plus any and all laws he deemed unnecessary or created laws as he wished. This exists in my mind as he is an evil man, not worthy in any way to be trusted with any role in anyway within all our government. Moreover it's sad we are exposed to his corrupt manifestation whatsoever, with all of the circumstances I am questioning WHY has this matter evolved without Obama's impeachment.

One should by necessity refocus their attendtion on the present difficulties facing us now, at this moment and how we should confront these adversities. I am a firm believer in the idea our constitution is NOT a living document, growing to satisfy a lethargic public and a ravenous government. I be obliged by necessity have to refocus my attendtion on the present difficulties facing us now, at this moment and how we should confront these adversities.

I am a firm believer in the proposition that our constitution is NOT a living document, growing to satisfy a lethargic public and a ravenous government. It's just an assertion which has been passed along by many who elected to postulated "let's keep up with the times" unfortunately an argument poorly chosen.

Provoking words spoken by men of remarkable wisdom, courage and comprehending the need for and having faith in God giving them the innermost spirit needed to struggle on and the audacity to take on the British military. These was the men, the founders of our Republic and constructing a constitution like none other.
Below you will read some of their words.

## Part One Plus

As George Washington stated; *"Let us with caution indulge the supposition that morality can be maintained without religion. Whatever may be conceded to the influence of refined education, reason and experience both forbid us to expect national morality can prevail in exclusion of religious principle".* One other quote from the founders of our Constitution, Benjamin Franklin; "Only a virtuous people are capable of freedom. As a nation becomes corrupt and vicious, they have need of masters". Thomas Jefferson; *"On every question of construction let us carry ourselves back to the time when the Constitution was adopted, recollect the spirit manifested in the debates, and instead of trying what meaning may be squeezed out of the text or invented against it, conform to the probable one in which it was passed".*
*To suppose that any form of government will secure liberty or happiness without any virtue in the people is a chimerical idea.* James Madison
*The sum of it... is, if we would most truly enjoy the gift of Heaven, let us be a virtuous people; then shall we both deserve and enjoy it. If failing we shall not enjoy it, Though the form of our constitution carries the face of the most exalted freedom, in reality be the most abject slaves.* Samuel Adams

Again Senate Republicans were attempting to ascertain how former Secretary of State Hillary Clinton's top assistant Huma Abedin, was allowed to keep working at the State Department under a special, part-time status while also being employed at a politically-connected consulting firm, according to news reports on Saturday. Questions also linger about Ms. Abedin's alleged connection to the Muslim Brotherhood's women's auxiliary while having access to classified information and documents.

Iowa GOP Sen. Chuck Grassley, chairs the Senate Judiciary Committee and following up allegations that both women had used the private Internet server and email

24

accounts. Both were for State Department correspondence, even those that were considered confidential and classified. Grassley claims that the earlier requests were sent to the department and have largely come to remain ignored, since the Senate was then controlled by the Democrats. Now with the GOP in the majority new requests have gone to the department's inspector general and to Secretary of State John Kerry, seeking their involvement. I expect that request to die a certain death.

What also made it difficult was the fact that during Clinton's time as Secretary of State, her department was without an Inspector General for quite a long period of time. Grassley's first probe began in 2013, when he requested all communications between Abedin, after she went from being a full-time assistant chief of staff for Clinton to a part-time assistant chief of staff. The reason for the changes was that Huma began her job with the government consulting company, Tenneco.

Senate Republicans are renewing efforts to learn why Huma Abedin, a top assistant to Secretary of State Hillary Clinton, why she was allowed to stay at the agency under a special part-time status, moreover being employed at a politically-connected consulting firm.

New requests had been rendered by Sen. Chuck Grassley, following the revelations that both women had used the private Internet server. Sen. Grassley said the earlier requests had been largely ignored, so trusting when the new requests arrive they will have greater impact on Secretary of State John Kerry, therefore by seeking his far deeper involvement, Grassley is expecting it to give rise to sounder conclusions plus pronounced solutions.

Hillary Clinton's longtime aide Huma Abedin's ties to the Muslim Brotherhood are well documented and well known to Clinton and to other Washington insiders, such as Republican Senator John McCain, who defended Abedin in a speech on the Senate floor when five conservative Members of the House of Representatives called for the State Department Inspector General to look into Abedin's fitness to hold a high level security clearance while she served as Hillary Clinton's deputy chief of staff at the State Department.

Observers have called the Clinton email scandal an unprecedented breach of national security and that it has been revealed that Huma Abedin is a central figure in the national security scandal. Now disaster wrought by the compromise of military and diplomatic intelligence sent and received through Hillary Clinton's unsecured private email server, is there really no precedent for Abedin's role in this disaster?

A July 2013, letter from the department to Grassley, provided by the senator's office, states Abedin worked full-time from January 2009 to June 2012. It also states Abedin did not list herself as being employed outside and shown upon the required record.

The most recent available federal documents show the rate as $74.51 per hour with a maximum pay of $155,500 annually. A number of conflict-of-interest concerns arise when a government employee is simultaneously being paid by a private company, especially when that company is Tenneco, Grassley said in the March 19 letter to Kerry that also raised concerns about Abedin and other department employees appearing to have been "improperly categorized" as special government employees, or SGEs.

Grassley says he specifically wants to know "what steps the department took to ensure that … Abedin's outside employment with political intelligence and corporate advisory, failed to explain why it was not conflicting with her simultaneous employment at the State Department."

The letter to department Inspector General Steve Lonick also questions whether the department's "excessive" use of SGE designations undermines ethics standards and if Clinton and Abedin's private emails have the potential to impede the department from fulfilling Freedom of Information Act, or FOIA, requests, over which the upper chamber's Judiciary Committee has legislative jurisdiction.

Grassley says the department's answers have so far been "largely unresponsive" and points to a November 2014 response that in part states "an individual may receive an SGE designation if he or she is joining the department from the private sector or is coming from another government position."

While she's probably best known as the wife of the disgraced politician Anthony Weiner, 36-year-old Huma Abedin an Islamic follower leads quite a life, her eclectic background is very interesting. Currently, she works for Hillary Clinton as the former First Lady figures out what she wants to do next in her political life.

Let's start with Huma Abedin's nationality. Since she was born in Kalamazoo, Michigan, that automatically makes her a United States citizen. That is true even though she spent the vast majority of her childhood in Saudi Arabia.

As for race, one would question, because her father is from India and her mother is from Pakistan. It also makes her ethnicity being Pakistani-Indian. Considering these are neighboring countries, this mix isn't too unusual.

This lovely lady was raised Muslim and continues to practice the religion even though Weiner is Jewish. In addition to English, she also speaks Urdu (the national language of Pakistan) and Arabic (the official language of Saudi Arabia).

Obama and Janet Napolitano appointed devout Muslim to Homeland Security Post, Arif Alikhan from the Muslim brotherhood as Assistant Secretary for Policy Development.

Source of the announcement: Homeland Security Press Room.

Kareem Shora, who was born in Damascus, Syria was appointed by DHS Secretary Napolitano as Homeland Security Advisory Council (HSAC)

Washington, DC June 5, 2009

The American-Arab Anti-Discrimination Committee (ADC) was proud to announce at a ceremony held in Albuquerque, New Mexico, DHS Secretary Janet Napolitano swore-in ADC National Executive Director Kareem Shora as a member of the Homeland Security Advisory Council (HSAC).

Devout Muslims being appointed to critical Homeland Security positions? Was it not men of the "Devout Muslim Faith" that flew planes into U.S. buildings not too long ago? What the heck is this president thinking? It is my personal opinion Obama knows precisely what he was embarking upon.

The first member on the list is Arif Alikhan, who has been serving in the Department of Homeland Security (DHS) since 2006.

DHS head Janet Napolitano appointed Alikhan , Assistant Secretary for Policy Development.

Imam Mohamed Magid naturalized citizen who immigrated to the United States from the Sudan in 1987. In 2011 President Barack Obama appointed Magid to serve in a Countering Violent Extremism Working Group with the DHS. On January 22, 2013 Magid took part in the inaugural ceremonies of President Obama but the White House has no Sharia Czar, a title given to Iman Magid by critics of the Obama Administration. In 2007 Alikhan was instrumental in removing the Muslim terror tracking plan in LA. The Muslim 'Mapping' Plan of the Los Angeles Police Department is now "dead on arrival" according to Chief William Bratton. "It is over and not just put on the side,"

Chief Bratton in a meeting with the Muslim leadership of Southern California, at that time was moderated by Arif Alikhan. Chief Bratton acknowledged the hurt and offense caused to Muslims and agreed to send a letter to the Muslim community announcing the official termination of the 'mapping' plan.

"I would be very worried, both for the United States and its friends in the region, like Israel, about the implications of any substantial involvement by Elbaradei in setting Egyptian national policy," warns John Bolton, the former United States Ambassador to the United Nations, who had extensive dealings with the Egyptians as a U.N. official.

ElBaradei headed the U.N's International Atomic Energy Agency, or I.A.E.A., 12 years. It was in that role that some accused him of being biased toward Iran, though he denied it. He had a stormy relationship with the George W. Bush administration, which tried to block his reappointment as head of the agency in 2005.

Critics accused ElBaradei of sometimes seeming to give Tehran the benefit of the doubt, and downplaying a possible military aspect to its nuclear program despite what the U.S. and others said was evidence to the contrary.

Less than a year and a half ago, ElBaradei told the Council on Foreign Relations in New York, that "we have no indications, no concrete proof that Iran has an ongoing nuclear weapons program. That is my view.

Then critics, like former Ambassador Bolton, fault him. "He is one of those fashionable anti-American international leftists. He's already criticized the United States for its policy in Egypt this week, and he announced in his previous presidential campaign that he would recognize Hamas and end sanctions against Hamas, which presumably means opening the Egyptian border with the Gaza Strip. He has also said the Muslim Brotherhood in Egypt is not an extremist organization."

But the inspector told Bolton Mohamed ElBaradei believed that as top U.N. official, he had a moral responsibility to be objective, and impartial no matter what the critics say. ElBaradei now shed the role as he marches with protestors on the Cairo streets.

Wiladat e Muhammadi also took aim at his imagined enemies, saying: One of the greatest social ills facing Americans today is Islamophobia and anti-Muslim bigotry. And if you trace the organizations and the main advocates and activists in Islamophobia in America, you will see that all those organizations are pro-Israeli occupation organizations and activists.

Cairo Hamas and Muslim Brotherhood are all terrorists, along with their 100 front organizations. Just google "the project Muslim brotherhood" for truth and facts. The Islam Caliphate will eventually come to America, unless good men and women prevent it from happening. It is almost impossible today to tell any difference between so called peaceful Islam and peaceful Mosques due to the practice of "Taqivya" that is found in the Quran. If anyone can explain the difference, please let me know.

We have yet to learn from the tragedy of 9/11. After over a decade of violence and terror from Islam, it has not been resolved. Ayaan Hirsi Ali perhaps said it best, "Violence is inherent in Islam". It must be noted that Ayaan has won every single debate on the subject as to whether or not Islam is a religion of peace. It is not. She speaks from experience as a former Muslim, and speaks out against radical Islam and Sharia Law. She has been accused of hate speech and has death threats on her life, merely for telling the truth.

Did you know that Anwar Awlaki was thought to be a moderate Muslim by our own government? There was a time when our government thought that Anwar Awlaki (American born terrorist and Iman preacher at a Virginia Mosque and main recruiter for al Qaeda) was a moderate Muslim, and actually invited him to speak to members of Congress and our military officers. Now we have over 2450 Mosques and climbing rapidly.

He had fooled them all, or perhaps our government is lying again using Taqiyya (The practice of concealing one's beliefs in dangerous circumstances), originates in the Qur'an, which deems blameless those who disguise their beliefs in such cases.

The practice of Taqiyya in difficult circumstances is considered legitimate by Muslims of various sects. Practically, Taqiyya is any form of lying, deceit, misleading, half-truths or related practices condoned by Islamic doctrine to further the growth of Islam or to protect the individual from harm. Taqiyya is one of the reasons we are "surprised" by acts of violence or terror from those previously considered of being a "moderate" Muslim.

He was an American born terrorist who incited English speaking Muslims to commit terrorist acts. He preached to 3 of the 9/11 hijackers and was linked with Nidal Hassan who committed the Fort Hood massacre. Awlaki preached a hateful ideology and inciting violence against America and a leader of Al Qaeda.

A good friend of Anwar Awlaki is Islim Suhaib Webb who worked alongside of Awlaki and also joined al Qaeda. Where do you think Ism Sahib Webb is today, almost too shocking to believe but he teaches the future of Muslim leadership in America, at a college in Claremont California? This school strangely named Bayan College has recently participated in a Social Media workshop at Winter School (Bayan known for Honest Man?). We are the first college in Oman to offer degrees in Media studies, and are located in Central Muscat, the heart of Oman's prominent Media Industry. Our programs include Journalism, Broadcasting and Public Relations. How pathetic and perhaps dangerous this can become? Our P.C. attitude could become part of our down fall. (Please excuse my indulgence in Arabic spelling.)

Why he was even allowed back into the United States for his known terrorist connections, why was he not arrested let alone teaching at a college? He apparently has convinced the government that he is a moderate Muslim, (will we never learn that for Islam it's OK to lie?). Google "the project Muslim brotherhood" their doctrine to destroy America from within by stealth jihad, lies and deception just like Anwar Awlaki, who had the majority of our government convinced, he was just a moderate Muslim. Anwar Awlaki, the leader of Al Qaeda was killed in a drone attack and it was authorized by President Obama on 9/20 2011.

The mainstream news has no idea that this man "Islam Suhaib Webb" is now teaching at Bayan College, nor do they care. Also on the staff, is Salam Al Marryat, who has defended terrorist acts and the groups that carry them out. Dr. Asifa Qureshi Landis who defends the Sharia law is also on the staff.

All are so called Islam scholars and moderates just like Anwar Awlaki led us to believe. The fact remains that this college should be investigated, plus the entire faculty investigated. What kind of peaceful moderate Muslim leaders are being taught there? We need to see what is really being taught, before we have another "clone" of Anwar Awlaki in America.

The recent release of the 5 Taliban Terrorist leaders will cause more Americans to die as they will continue to plot another 9/11 where they left off. Just one more stupid decision by our government, it will be the major mistake of the 21st Century, to have released these savage Taliban "monsters", now more Americans will die as a direct result of this decision. This by deliberate action President Obama, who should be impeached for his past treasonous proceedings, now we face another.

I could mention our "open borders" that are bringing in more terrorists daily, to eventually attack us, but that is a whole other subject.

Al Qaeda and the Taliban are alive and well creating havoc throughout the World. How many more people will be slaughtered by them? It is another Holocaust killing innocent children, and infidels, Christians, Jews, and priests, and anyone that stands in their way of the Caliphate. There were over 1.3 million Christians in Iraq, Iran, Syria, Egypt and Lebanon, now there are less than 300,000.

Where is the World uproar and condemnation of these barbaric, killer savages? They must be stopped now. Why aren't We the People pressing the Congress we placed in office, to respond to the needs identified by the actions of these barbarians deposited in front of them, this includes Barack Obama. This vile man is acting out his best to provide the Iranians with nuclear weapons. As Sect. of State Kerry flies from place to place, actually globetrotting, as negotiations seem to grow more complex as each day passes. Furthermore, why have Christians become absent, worst comatose, I persist in asking, where is our faith in God Almighty, He will not fail us if we are down on our knees. We may seek one, but there is no other answer.

The complexities seem to evolve from the Iranians, amusing themselves at our expense, while Obama must dole out bits and pieces with an attempt to placate a republican Congress, who are themselves with only a slight idea where they stand on this situation. While congress dithers the Iranians grow bolder in their position regarding their nuclear ambitions. The leaders of Iran have the gall to dictate to the world how the conditions of their nuclear operation will proceed. I previously questioned why are we negotiating with them, rather how we should demand any nuclear programs, begins with why they have need. At this immediate juncture, while I'm writing these words, Sect. of State Kerry is negotiating with Iran, excuse me, negotiating again, why are we negotiating with the most terrorist nation in the world? Merely because Obama's desire has driven him to grant the capacity for the Iranians, the interval needed to build a nuclear bomb, as in that event would extremely determinedly set the entire Middle East, totally on fire.

In my simple, while even so basic a mind for examining foreign affairs, nevertheless, discover it my judgement, in Obama's pathological mentality, that of such an uncontrolled person shall bring chaos to America and to our reliable and trustworthy allies, the Israelis. We ought to act quickly as time is presently briefer than we might have assumed a few months ago. I am of the opinion, better yet convinced that we must return to the God our founders were believers in God. Now the situation grows far worse which requires greater measures on the part of Christians and especially Christian leaders, it is incumbent for those who say they are Christians to pick up the pace, take the necessary measures by pressing their representatives not to accept any negotiations whatsoever with Iran. Let's pursue and inspire them to have sufficient courage to set Obama down. I encourage you to remember this, our nation was built on the separation of powers and congress being one, must exercise those powers.

As citizens of this nation, a nation designed on the idea that a union of many diversified states, yet each sovereign could work together, for the benefit of each other. I am still certain this is true, believing this design was inspired by God, thus will not fail if properly administered. It is an indisputable fact, there are millions of citizens who think and have faith in the same God. We by choice have chosen leaders in congress who must support these ideals and are obliged to meet the task.

It is we as a people, who essentially are the impetus that is necessary to perform the required execution for a reversal of direction this nation of ours ought to travel. We cannot wait for some luminary or superstar, in fact nor anyone else who may happen along and then by some mysterious means guide us through the Nile River and leading us out of captivity, frivolously speaking. Let's face it there's just you and I, we are believing He would assist them in their efforts to acquire their security and freedom from England's King George.

I am most certainly sure, the situation is considerably worse today than in the occurrence of the revolutionary war, generally the leaders and men driving the event, those who's duty and obligation are required to meet the objective. I'm sorry, however there is no delegation, there's you, your neighbor, your brother and/or sister, you must have gotten the point, we each and every one to whom appreciates the quest should participate in some way. Least of all pressure your congress person, remember they work for you and your interest and your safety, it's your money they spend, government has no money, seldom produces anything except problems.

I firmly believe it is the Christians and their leader's responsibility to inspire, while at the very least a stimulating, provocative requirement, yet not bellicose, merely an exhortation aimed at our leaders and their actions.

Consequently many so called Christians say pray, God will take care of these problems, prayer is surely indispensable, however while our brothers and sisters are brutalized in the Middle East we must respond to protect them. Necessity requires a call for the barbarians' responsible, most essential be eliminated by whatever force required. As Dr. Jeffress of the 1st Baptist Church of Houston Texas, in his opinion most pastors and or Christian leaders are wimps, they will not speak to the issues destroying America and now to the genocide of Christians conducted around the world. He and a few others believe prayer first then annihilation of the barbarians, I too believe in this objective, as there is none other.

It is the weakness of bible believing Christians in which I reason have allowed this true holocaust to exist. Furthermore, I have ruminated over my own thinking and am able to see the process of damage and obvious intent to extinguish our faith in God. This within the nation conceived by Godly men to whom followed His precepts, thus creating this unique nation of ours.

Now there are many inside our society and government who's esoteric schemes to destroy the very basis of our nation, sadly so many passive Christians fail to realize what's happening and may not much care, nor are they willing to protest against those denying our God and attempting to destroy our faith. This contrary to the constitution they swore to uphold, even such as Keith Ellison who swore on the Qur'an, and the head of the CIA Mr. Brennan took the oath given by vice President Joe Biden, on a version of the Constitution, without the FIRST amendment, that among others. This on its face appears impossible to me, that we as a people, Christian or not, would accept such a conflict of ideology, yet this battle has been drawn. The question remains, whether true Christians are prepared, as God has equipped us and is more than ready to buttress those willing to engage.

We have experienced a venture through our history, woefully a mere seventy years and our priorities have fallen away, succumb to a man using the negro to advance his personal agenda. Thus we are now reaching into today, including our current trials, anxieties and wide ranging difficulties facing our nation. The deterioration of our society, in most cases without a feeling of necessity for change, yet poverty, privation and indigence at a historic high.

All branches of government are characteristically corrupt, even the Supreme Court of the United States, its Chief Justice John Roberts lied in the important decisions considering health care. The ramifications of this candid lawsuit will be felt even today, more so many years to come. Having three branches of government so designed by the creators of the constitution to maintain check on one another. The result of money along with corruption of power, resulted in the chaos we are living today. If it weren't in lieu of greed and hunger for power, the nation could have been that proverbial beacon on the hill. Instead we find ourselves being starved for trust by our friends and deprived of fear by our enemies, immeasurably to our demise.

In this short dissertation I have endeavored to demonstrate how easily man is corrupted, perhaps not necessarily money or power, though our desires for more, bigger and better things are a weakness, it seems we all enjoy and to some extent having worked for them, feel they are fair game, thus perhaps it's the overdoing we indulge ourselves. However at this point we must by commitment turn ourselves around and demand government do likewise.

A moment ago I spoke of Chief Justice John Roberts and his propensity for deceit, costing the citizens of the nation multi-billions of dollars and contributing to the social decline of our republic, still reeling from the impact. Thomas Jefferson once stated in the Declaration of Independence *"when a long train of abuses and usurpations, pursuing invariably the same object evinces a design to reduce them under absolute despotism, it is their right, it is their duty, to throw off such government, and to provide new guards for their future security.* Such has been the patient sufferance of these colonies"*, I could change colonies to states. These colonists were willing to defy England, going to war over similar difficulties, taxation without representation, inflicting their preferences, loss of liberty and uttermost, losing their freedom of choice to worship as they pleased.

35

I have read the transcripts of these cases involved around The Affordable Care Act and the arguments presented by the government (defendants) and by the plaintiff's listed below:

The following arguments I had undertaken two years ago, I find it reasonable to once again use these arguments in this little book to illustrate a corrupt government, at its highest level.

Case 11- ***National Federation of Independent Business, et***

393      ***al., , v. Kathleen Sebelius, Secretary of Health and***

           ***Human Services, et al.,***

Case 11- ***Department of Health and Human Services, et al.,*** 398

           ***v. Florida, et al.***

Case      ***Florida, et al., v. Department of Health and Human*** 11-400

***Services, et al.***

.

All three of these cases make up the authentic fundamentals of the Affordable Care Act, heard by the Supreme Court of the United States, verdict in June of 2012. I have established my opinion by *Fiat Justitia ruat coelom,* after a long and questioning study, by using their own offered and existing court cases against them, plus simple logic using the true meaning of words they have injected improperly, especially words misused in a particular era.

It is the determination of this exercise to expose the highest court in our nation and its willingness to excel in corruption, plus an ability to find the need and fell into its degenerate practices, very sad. I have taken this challenge seriously and with somber but with aggressive prosecution.

This entire little book is not a religious undertaking, rather a call for responsible, true Christians to support the Congressman they elected, if he or she is corrupt fire them. The founders realized that our faith in God needed to be paramount, individually and collectively as a nation and above all <u>any</u> government. Hence we have a secular government under God, separate and apart from our faith in God. However it is particularly incumbent upon Christians praying and also robustly participating. Please remember our nation was designed as Christian, hence it belongs to our republic, now it's up to Christians to return our republic toward submission to God's essentials fundamentals, thus receiving our guidance from God. I am sorry as we should move on but...

At this time I sense a need to describe the difference between a republican form of government and a democracy, "A democracy is nothing more than mob rule, where 51 percent of the people may take away the rights of the other 49", so stated Thomas Jefferson. I am of the opinion that the so called federal government is not an entity and is without soveriegnty unless this body is comprised by a union of elected persons from the fifty sovereign states. All power which may be given this body was granted by the sovereign states and its power is enumerated in our Constitution, it has no existence lacking the persons elected in each state coming together in union, creating a House of Representatives and Senate. All members are citizens from the individual fifty states and speak on behalf of and for their respective constituents, thus creating a body politico called the federal government. This body receives its authority from the Ninth and Tenth amendments and the fact our Constitution was written by the orginal thirteen sovereign states, therefore they are seated in the bounds of that authority.

Consequently, the President and vice President are elected by electors, again selected by the citizens from each state, hence each state is afforded electors according to their population. If a candidate receives the positive amount of votes in a particular state, he or she gains all the electors from that state. I merely hope this simple explanation of a Republic, defines for you the difference between a Democratic and Republican form of government.

Now our republic is befallen to a paradox, thus where those we have chosen to become representative of our interest are basically interested in their reelection, at least for the most part. In the initial years of the young republic, the idea was representatives would be chosen from amongst their area, this would produce a person with the necessary knowledge to best speak and vote on their behalf, plus the person chosen could be a baker, carpenter, store owner, barber, etc., and during their service return to enlighten their constituents and receive additional input from them. After serving he or she would return to their previous occupation and shall be compensated for their time spent in service of the people. Relatively, today it has developed into a full time occupation where the income is more than two hundred thousand dollars a year plus countless perks and great retirements, I am without knowledge where the idea of a retirement salary originated, for certain not the Constitution.

There are 2,748,978 civilian federal employees in the United States as of January 2009. This is according to the Federal Employment Statistics published by the U.S. Office of Personnel Management. Employees with security agencies (CIA, NSA, etc), as well as the National Imagery and Mapping Agency are not included in this number. Of that number 97.6% of civilian federal employees work in the executive branch of government. It is hard to imagine, President Obama's additional increased in staff and his staff require approximately 3 million plus people in order to keep our republic moving.

In addition there are 24, 000 staff workers, about thirty five staff persons for each person in Congress, what's more this seems an over abundant amount as they refuse to accomplish the smallest of necessities our republic requires. This is not a problem of one party, rather a bankruptcy of both parties, a collapse in their responsibility to those who have chosen them to work on their behalf. The Supreme Court has again lied, used deception and convolution plus twisting of words in a most significant issue of subsides, changing a law stating State exchanges were entitled to help certain persons with their health insurance cost. Perhaps I repeat, but this is an essential issue.

This found in the following portion of the act: **HEALTH PLAN, A PART OF SECTION 1401 (Generally called subsides)**

At (2), (A):

(1) IN GENERAL. The term 'premium *assistance* credit amount' means, with respect to any taxable year, the sum of the premium assistance amounts determined under paragraph with respect to all coverage months of the taxpayer occurring during the taxable year.

(2) PREMIUM ASSISTANCE AMOUNT A premium assistance amount determined under this subsection with respect to any coverage month is the amount equal to the lesser of—

(A) the monthly premiums for such month for 1 or more qualified health plans offered in the **individual market within a State** which cover the taxpayer, the taxpayer's spouse, or any dependent (as defined in section 152) of the taxpayer and which were enrolled in through an

**Exchange established by the State** under 1311 of the Patient Protection and Affordable Care Act.

The Supreme Court stated that the Congress misplaced a few words and there were drafting errors, such as the words **individual market within a State,** and one could add **Exchange established within a State**, please note the capital S used in this statue, specifically denoting one of the fifty States which were enrolled in State exchanges, these words sound clear to me.

There were no drafting errors, no misplaced words. Only these architects reached a reckless, strategic decision, their dangling of federal subsidies as the reward for a State assuming the costs of running an exchange. The ploy was adverse, excessive and risky. Though if successful, it would allow the feds to unload the cost of exchanges to the states, while state politicians could claim credit for reducing the sticker shock of the insurance it markets. Oklahoma and 35 other states weren't interested. The fact is Obama got exactly what he wanted, only it didn't go as planned. So now it was up to the Supreme Court to fix the problem, and they did what was necessary, the law and Constitution be dammed. This corrupt reasoning, without Constitutional law or ideology is called "Judicial Deference", an idea brought into the courts after Chief Justice Marshall's decision in 1803 concerning the Marbury vs Madison case.

Irrespective of law the Supreme Court decided to defy all logic with Justice John Roberts leading the parade of corrupt men and women in black robes, declining to follow the law rather choosing to create law. Thus another chapter in their twisting of words and in some case going as far as replacing them completely. In the infamous words of John Roberts, one must do all possible to save an act intended by Congress, regardless of the Constitution. I find just the opposite opinion by President Thomas

Jefferson's statement regarding such. I am paraphrasing, "warning not to attempt to expand the meaning of the law, keep it in the spirit and time it was written, plus never attempt squeezing it in order to get more out than from which it was intended." Food for thought, more from Thomas Jefferson, "I tremble for my country when I reflect that God is just, that His justice cannot sleep forever".

Which brings me to the next case with their decision released the following day, the same sex marriage issue, being passed with a five to four outcome. This in favor of preventing the states from stopping or impeding same sex marriage. Strange that now Justice Roberts is choosing the absolute opposite position, he now is of the opinion that the law must be followed, as this is paramount and failing to do so would be unconstitutional. The results of these two Supreme Court decisions will reverberate through the core of our republic, bringing new grief and distress to a heretofore overburdened populace. Furthermore moving farther away from God and the need to follow His moral standards, which will bring about a significant detrimental change and decline to our nation.

Returning to the original premise of part one from this little book, leading to the exposing of government corruption at its highest level, the Supreme Court of the United States. This exercise bringing to bear the profound willingness of government to defraud, deceive and betray in order to maintain the will of Congress and/or the President, as today the three branches of government are united as one, to create the loss of freedom, liberty and sovereignty for the states and its people. This situation didn't come about without the assistance of the people to facilitate a so called democracy, actually socialism with an opportunity to vote for which socialist, now the entire Democratic Party is just that, socialistic, this ideology is where you have no clear choice.

Therefore, it brings into view the fact it's the people which ultimately define how our government functions and chooses how a nation moves forward, or more often retreats into chaos. The lack of these facts are to my mind, appear to point toward absolute socialism, though many of our time-consuming, prolonged engagements in the polititical system, cry conservatism, rather their obvious actions prove their interest to be otherwise, self- indulgence.

The creation of this fact is the lack of the people and each citizen to have some involvement, even a small portion in their government and I will again say, especially those who call themselves Christian people. It is not enough to spout the name of Christ and fail to lead in the effort to maintain our republic, as it was originally designed by God and wise men at least recognizing the God of the Christianity and installing His values into our Constitution. Which gave this republic a Christian basis, the foundation on which to build this young nation, who's people are free to conduct themselves, with liberty, freedom and pursue happiness as they decide.

Then the citizens select from amongst themselves, persons to represent them for a period of time in their own government, receiving their just powers from those they govern.

This is the essence of our Constitution pure and simple, rather today we find university students accepting the idea our First Amendment should be repealed. Thus would in fact destroy the firm guarantee of freedom of our faith, free speech, a free press and our right to peaceably petition the government. All have and are under the threat of OUR NATIONAL government, the most important being our faith in God Almighty, strange as it may seem, since He is our only redeeming strength and simply the solitary answer to the nations degeneration, both as individual society and the elected political creatures leading us into chaos. We as Christians are obligated to pray for God's guidance, that our people again will begin believing in God Almighty. As astute men, who with God Almighty's wisdom and strength, created this Christian republic. The preamble exemplifies the ideas and considerations for the soveriegn states purpose of joining together in unification.

*"We the People of the United States, in Order to form a more perfect Union, establish Justice, insure domestic Tranquility, provide for the common defense, promote the general Welfare, and secure the Blessings of Liberty to ourselves and our Posterity, do ordain and establish this Constitution for the United States of America".*

These simple words were all which were necessary and essential for an explanation of the following Constitution of the United States, our republic a Christian sovereign body of persons.

James Madison, the fourth president, known as The Father of Our Constitution made the following statement *"We have staked the whole of all our political institutions upon the capacity of mankind for self-government, upon the capacity of each and all of us to govern ourselves, to control ourselves, to sustain ourselves according to the Ten Commandments of God."*

Patrick Henry, that patriot and Founding Father of our country said, *"It cannot be emphasized too strongly or too often that this great nation was founded not by religionists but by Christians...not on religions but on the Gospel of Jesus Christ".* These words are all which are necessary and were indispensable to bring into being a Christian republic of sovereign states in unanimity.

Now examining our republic we find insatiability in the majority of persons, self-indulgence with little concern for others, this includes Christians who have very little significant time for a genuine effort to reach others for Christ and/or involve themselves in activities around which is God centered. As for myself I believe Christians are obliged to lead in the policies and political issues confronting our Republic. In our Republic it's Christians who identify with the God who created and continues sustaining all of humankind, our failure to comprehend this duty, has given us the many Godless leaders of today and most of those who wish to following them.

This appears to me as an example of an exceedingly proportioned foolishness, by "We the foolish People", rather than the independent and Christian "We the People". We at this time, are in midst of a presidential election, reading and listening to the news media, I failed to hear or read little of the cataclysmic crisis facing us, the drug epidemic as the ultimate issue confronting our Republic, nonetheless undeclared by any candidate. I will say the media has presented special exposure on this subject and our government officals seem by a great extent, having ignored this severe life-threatening matter. Nevertheless, as one individual I believe it should be paramont, to

42

our elected congress, thus becoming more focused, producing a greater effort, a more profound endeavor on halting the influx and manufacturing of all illicit drugs.

It is the young people who, for the most part are affected, yet we seem awed by their actions and life styles. Bernie Sanders has gotten their attention and responsiveness, this due to the free things he promised, instead of course he could not produce. Though it's not only the young, relatively people of all incomes, ages, races and polotics. This evil is about money, the income for so many persons all over our Republic.

This epidemic sweeping the country at this point is uncontrolled, and is without concern enough to become a major issue by the candidates. Again I ask, where do we find these so called Christians?

It may border on the perception that I am selecting Christians to point out their failures, of course that's true, as Christians are far more responcable to become involved in matters of this serious substances. It is my concern which causes me to assert such questions, forgive me if you find me to bold.

At this point I find it necessary to challenge some justices in the Supreme Court of our government. Those associate Justices, in particular Chief Justice John Roberts, convoluting or creating new law at their discretion

Consequently, in so doing you will observe the justices most often in disagreement along party lines, rather than that of the constitution.

## Part Two

### Government's Creation of Parity, Their intended Warped and Perverted View of our Republic, the Supreme Court as an example.

The following document was built on the deceitful activities of the highest court in our republic, as I felt an inner influence and a motivation to show the depths of corruption our republic has submerged itself, into itself. As a people today, we generally operate exclusive of God, thus as a consequence a government socialistic to the core and soon to become fascism like, moreover with regards to our republic only its vestiges remain. The Affordable Care Act is so deceitfully and inadequately organized, that lies are now supplementary to the act, in a colossal fashion. The health insurance in our nation today demands major changes, however never intended to unleash the U.S. government upon it, like any dog turned loose, highly appealing to all that red meat (taxes).

My point remains, while chasing after the truth, is twofold, first to expose Justice John Roberts and some of his cohorts, for distorting and/or, defying our Constitution in engagements never seen before, merely to satisfy a socialist President, House, and Senate all the while destroying our Republic. The meaning of words were changed or twisted beyond recognition. Secondly, I hope as others have tried to educate We the People, in the need for returning to God and to the ideals embedded by our Founding Fathers. As the way a peoples government, where many moving parts are controlled, through inspection and direction, from the bottom up, by We the People, seeking God's guidance. The following arguments at issue with Chief Justice John Roberts amongst others in the U.S. Supreme Court are reflective of our government, exhibited currently these days. In fact most have heard the phrase "legislating from the bench", this case is a perfect example, as the legislators wanted taxes rather than penalty so stated by law. The court henceforth accommodated by changing the meaning of the word penalty to tax, as the legislators wished they had written, trying to explain was

45

quite a task. Therefore, I have chosen them as an example, to present for you the reader. This by *Fait Justitia /Justas Naturalis* Latin for "Let there be justice" and "*a legal inference as to the existence of truth and of a fact*".

I humbly desire some of my following arguments against this irresponsible act, are in some way helpful, explaining the level to which our government will stoop to support their agenda, if merely in resulting for a number of our people. May God scrutinize, then praying He bless my simple and straightforward words.

George Melcher… Citizen of New Mexico, Petitioner


Cases in question


Patient Protection and Affordable Care Act   I.R.S. code 1986 at 5000A
The following Cases- doc., 11-393, 11-398, 11-400


Vs


Chief Justice Roberts, Justices Ginsburg, Breyer, Sotomayor, Kagan

# My Opening Remarks

After reading the Supreme Courts' decision regarding the Affordable Health Care Act, unfortunately a misuse of congresses taxing power, thus inappropriately becoming an exaction. As a consequence, for myself as a Christian to challenge our government, under the authority of the First Amendment section four, "*to petition the government for a redress of grievance*", especially the Supreme Court and one Chief Justice John Roberts, among others in that supposedly august body. It has become obvious and necessary, that someone challenge or at the very least, questions as to the foundation for the mandate, the power to tax, which becomes the very heart of the mandate of this act. Case doc.no.11-398. The IRS code 1986 or Title 26, one in the same, at 5000A in IRS manual.

As a result of our administration's duplicity and its many absolute destructive actions, even as deceit prevails, we have taken upon ourselves the chore of exposing the illegitimacy of persons and entity. Passing laws which we the people are the recipients, laws of endless debt, hostile to our future, our children's, and perhaps our children's children. Having taken the task as a Christian patriot, to become bold and audacious enough to challenge five of the nine wise persons in the Supreme Court of these United States, our republic. Fervently I ascertained flaws, weakness and in some cases outright deception, but for the most part wishing truth being brought forward to the people. As the unscrupulous Nancy Pelosi stated "*you must first past the bill* (the affordable health care act)" *before you will understand it, in this fog of politics.*" Now some four and one half years later we are wiser. Not one representative read the appalling new law, 2700 plus pages, urgently pressed for passage by the representative from California's eighth district, Ms. Pelosi. Is my existence as a citizen not sufficient to be so bold as to ask why? While sitting there from her socialist perch, she drove the House of Representatives, many perhaps were merely concerned with their political positions. As they are only interested in positioning their future for the game of wild animals, mules vs. elephants. They promised the bill would be posted on the internet for 72 hours, of course I knew that was a falsehood, so without ado I printed a copy of all 2700 plus pages and sure as the sun rises in the east, less than 24 hours, puff it was gone, like smoke from a slow burning ember.

Then our imaginative Supreme Court had found a spurious way to perform the task presented them, without a whimper from the American people, including the Christian faithful, except for Justice Scalia, Kennedy, Thomas and Alito. Consequently, there goes our Christian republic deeper into socialism, devoid of a simple moan and with that a large challenge to Christianity.

It is my firm belief, as a true citizen of New Mexico one of fifty sovereign states, that my duty as a Christian patriot was to challenge Chief Justice John Roberts decision on these cases before them. I have found errors, lies and deception, truth stretching at its very least. His case law abstractions going back to Justice Marshall a Federalist, were used numerous times, yet none are possible.

Justice Marshall served from 1801 - 1835 and was instrumental in bringing the Constitution into an enhanced comprehension and the courts into a more equal status with the other two branches of government.

That being said, however he (John Roberts) moved the body politic to the liberal point of view, far from the ideas of Thomas Jefferson. The selection of the seat of the National government was chosen from (*soveriegn persons elected from soveriegn states and set in ten sq. miles*). Then these persons were sent to this area called Washington D.C., creating an area to exchange ideas, needs and helpful and necessary information. Not a retreat from state governments, therefore leading to the creation of a chasm between the states and national governments, not happening without the loss of states and the people's sovereignty.

Nevertheless, this seemed where John Roberts was most comfortable in his decisions, though he stresses his thinking is conservative. I find his use of positives all the while proving negatives, disturbing. His ability to use the narrowest of rules, even thinning them out further, trying to prove his point, most often devoid of any reason or Constitutional parallel.

This nation was founded on the principles established by God, as quoted in the document which gave validation for the creation of our Constitution, the Declaration of Independence. A phrase most often used, Life, Liberty and the pursuit of Happiness, the twelve preceding words are regularly forgotten words, they are absolute, "endowed by their creator with certain unalienable rights, that AMONG them are"... Life, Liberty and the pursuit of Happiness.

I wish to quote from James Madison *"Each state in ratifying the constitution, is considered a sovereign body independent of all others, and only to be bound by its own voluntary act. In this relation then, the new constitution will, if established, be a republic and not a national constitution."* I'm sorry but today it's an evolving, diminishing waste, nevertheless it lays there waiting for honest people to support it and government to obey.

Finally I expect to demonstrate how Justice Roberts brings into play a convoluted version of case law, plus excessive to the point of redundancy. Likewise his constant obstruction by the twisting of words and terms. This case isn't the subject of tax laws, but rather the Affordable Care Act, not of Health Care either, rather essentially an agenda with regards to insurance. All else is abstract bloviation, rhetorically bombastic deception by those persons, indicated by name in the following paragraph. At this point I will place on trial, actually a replicated trial, one Chief Justice Roberts, and Justice Ginsburg, Breyer, Sotomayor and Kagan, for what I believe, incompetence at best, or pure political lies, probability in conjunction.

Though my trial is presented as a similitude, in Latin (minor se majoram dixerit) it is scrupulously factual and genuine. Although one cannot prosecute these Justices, or impeach them at this time, they are as I have asserted, and will prove them to be guilty of corruption plus charlatans. All are guilty of corruption status, turning on a phrase called *Judicial Deference,* focused not on law, only the choice of words meaning as they arbitrarily declared and not necessarily at all as Noah Webster's definition, even to the point of converting the law through this action, therefore fitting their issue in this occasion. These mindsets have no legal grounds, simply without the ability to substantiate or corroborative laws, merely turning our Constitution into a worthless designed document, a powerless instrument.

 I pray God this will change soon, bringing hope for our Republic.

.

## Plaintiff's accusation Charge one

<u>Anti-Injunction Act</u>

The Anti-Injunction Act was thus being considered as a penalty, not as a tax by Chief Justice Roberts also, Justices Ginsburg, Breyer, Sotomayor, and Kagan. This was explicate, since it was clearly stated as a penalty and not a tax, then under the Anti-Injunction Act and because the individual mandate of Affordable Care Act <u>labeled</u> and argued by the government it was noted <u>a penalty,</u> hence one must assume it was penalty. The Anti-Injunction Act imposes a pay first, litigate later rule that is central to Federal tax, *what Federal tax* assessment and collection. The Act applies to essentially every tax penalty, *again what tax is penalized,* in the Internal Revenue Code at 5000A. There is no reason to think that Congress made a special exception for the <u>penalty</u> imposed by section 5000A. On the contrary, there are three reasons to conclude that the Anti-Injunction Act applies here.

First, Congress directed that the section 5000A <u>penalty</u> shall be assessed and collected in the same manner as taxes, *this statement is untrue.* Second, Congress provided that penalties are added to taxes for assessment purposes, *should read taxes are penalized for failure to properly pay taxes.* And third, the section 5000A <u>penalty</u> bears the key *indicia* of a tax. The word indicia means, (indications of the existence of a given fact*) nowhere in 5000A could indeed suggest a given fact to a key of a tax.*

The other four Justices, Scalia, Kennedy, Thomas and Alito also agreed but for other reasons. As the mandate was not a tax in the first place, plus having no bearing whatsoever on the label.

In the government's arguments, no less then eighteen (18) times, stating that it was a penalty in fact NOT a tax. Yet John Roberts continued to declare it a tax overriding the government's own position that it was a penalty and NOT a tax. As a citizen I find this quite incomprehensible and perplexing. What new tax has he created and from what source, and what label has he placed upon it, he chose no answers to the above questions.

Quote of Justice Roberts *"The Affordable Care Act requires that an applicable individual* (NOTE failing to define applicable individual) *failure to maintain essential coverage as a requirement may be <u>penalized</u>, this may reasonably be characterized as a tax, it is not my role to forbid it, or pass upon its wisdom or fairness."* Furthermore, John Roberts stated it was the courts duty for finding ways to support the law, affirming:

*"Though this court will often strain to construe legislation so as to save it against Constitutional attack"*. WHAT,… again he has it all wrong , rather it's the duty of the court to examine the law, considering how the law after reading the same, would that the statute be in accord with the characteristics within the framework of the Constitution, utterly and foremost. The framers intended for the Constitution to be the barrier to reign in wild and runaway legislatures. It's the framework of our Constitution, thus meant to be held to the highest in our republic.


**Justices dissenting, Justice Scalia, Kennedy, Thomas, Ali**to.

 The dissent takes issue with what it views as a jurisprudential novelty: They submitted, *"independently authorized, suggests the existence of a creature never hitherto seen in the United States Reports: A penalty for constitutional purposes that is also a tax for constitutional purposes. In all our cases the two are mutually exclusive"*.

Congress cannot pass something that is both a tax and a penalty, and the government cannot plead that it be considered as such because, as the dissent writes*, "the provision challenged under the Constitution is either a penalty or else a tax."* quote Justice Scalia

 **The dissent continues…**

*Of course in many cases what was a regulatory mandate enforced by a penalty, could have been imposed as a tax upon permissible action; or what was imposed as a tax upon permissible action could have been a regulatory mandate enforced by a penalty. But we know of no case, and the Government cites none, in which the imposition was, for Constitutional purposes, both. Thank you gentlemen. If I may be so presumptuous I would like to engender a thought with regards to the Tax Anti-Injunction act. As the act restrains one from executing an injunction, against the Internal Revenue Service until April of 2015, how does the court achieve its goal of passing judgment on any of the other issues, getting past the Anti- Injunction Act. It seems the Anti- Injunction act is dangling in space.*

Let us explore the words of admonition by one Thomas Jefferson and I quote those words for the court, as they seem to have forgotten or don't care as long as the body politic has been served, this unembellished statement bears repeating.

*"On every Question of the Construction let us carry ourselves back to the time when the Constitution was adopted, recollect the spirit manifested in the debates and instead of trying what meaning may <u>be squeezed out of the text, or invented against it,</u> conform to the probable one in which it was passed".*

Again I ask if the mandate is a penalty, rather than a tax, then how does the AntiInjunction act apply. This more than ever begs the question, how does the Supreme
Court apply an unknown, unanswered mandate to an unanswered Anti-Injunction act.

For me the whole question of the Affordable Care Act, which it is not, but merely a hoax. Had these needs been remanded to the states as the 9th and 10th requires, since the individual states are far more equipped for understanding, therefore able to meet the needs of their constituents. Hence by amending the Affordable Care Act, eliminating the I.R.S. Whee! Plus what a cost saving. The funds which the President will steal (716 billion), from the existing Medicare fund plus the I.R.S expenditure, plus the cost of the additional <u>Medicaid Act</u>, yet to be argued by the court. The accumulative funds (trillions of dollars) divided equally amongst the fifty states (not fifty-seven as the President erroneously imagines), according to their population. I included the below section of the arguments in the Supreme Court to show how capricious and whimsical their actions regarding time spent over the Anti-Injunction Act. Then it's your money their spending, I ask why should they care, plus their outcome was without merit on the face of it.

But standing between the Supreme Court and a politically charged decision upholding or striking down the mandate is a Reconstruction-era law, called the Tax AntiInjunction Act, which forbids lawsuits filed "*for the purpose of restraining the assessment or collection of any tax*" until that tax has been paid.

*The penalty is a tax because it will be paid at the same time as one's tax return.* This statement is again without merit on its face, yet fantastic for childlike thinking.

*The Tax Anti-Injunction Act would not prevail, if read as if the act as a penalty.* Confusion amongst the ranks?

The questions focused on how to wiggle out of the law's flat ban on tax-restraining lawsuits and how to avoid the conclusion that the mandate's penalty is, in fact, *a* tax. This was by no means a simple task.


Long (attorney for the state) told the justices that Congress said the *"penalty shall be assessed and collected in the same manner as taxes,"* but Justice Antonin Scalia suggested that courts owed no deference to that determination because, he said, *it was directed solely to the Treasury Department.* Justice Ruth Bader Ginsburg contrasted the Anti- Injunction Act's *"no suit ... shall be maintained"* language with that of a sister statute that expressly bans *"courts of the United States"* from delaying certain proceedings. This contrast, she contended, makes the Anti-Injunction Act *"Suitor directed in contrast to court-directed."* Never mind the rest of the statute, which reads,

*"in any court by any person."*

Then Justice Samuel Alito, for his part, implied that several past cases set the precedent that the "*Congress is not denominating it as a tax; it's denominating it as a penalty,*" Sotomayor said the penalty "*is not attached to a tax,*" Breyer said. "*It is attached to the health care requirement,*"

But Sotomayor asked, "*What's the parade of horrible, that would occur if the Anti-Injunction Act were something that the government could apply at its discretion"?* Long an "attorney" was not able to give a sufficient answer, so Scalia answered for him.

*"I will answer for him, if it were the government discretion, deciding how to apply the Anti-Injunction Act, where would it end".* We the People could be forced into buying anything or compulsory acting as we were told, NO FREEWILL.

"What'*s going to happen is you are going to have an intelligent federal court deciding whether you are going to make an exception?"* Scalia questioned.


With the high court apparently unanimously arrayed against the lawyer they had appointed to argue before them, Solicitor General Donald Verrilli and the challengers' lawyer, Gregory Katsas, were freed to tell the justices how to get past the Anti-Injunction Act.

Verrilli's main problem was getting past his own hair-splitting attempt to define "tax" to the government's benefit. The penalty is a tax for Constitutional purposes, he argued. Now looking ahead to the intricacies of Tuesday's debate.

Nevertheless, he said, it is not a tax under the Internal Revenue Code, which is what matters for the Anti-Injunction Act analysis.

Verrilli was asked "*today you are arguing that the penalty is not a tax,*" Justice Alito said. *"Tomorrow you are going to be back and you will be arguing that the penalty is a tax"*

Question, *"Has the Court ever held that something that is a tax for purposes of the taxing power under the Constitution is not a tax under the Anti-Injunction Act?"* Alito asked.

Verrilli said no.

A side note: Thomas Jefferson believed members of the Supreme Court should be elected as others serving in our republic and for a term, not for life. *Furthermore, they need to remember from whence our republic began, then undertake for which they were hired, applying the constitution to all laws consistently and equally.* These are the thoughts of a humble man as a result of a simple man's thinking.

These thoughts should be the basis for any court to discern any and all laws written by our legislators, today more than ever, after Nancy Pelosi's wild statement, *"pass it so you can read what's in it, away from the fog of controversy."* A noble idea Justice Roberts, pass the law and then YOU find a way to uphold it, categorization of the details in such a manner as to satisfy the legislators. What about the fact that you, nor the legislators have read this bill and how it might affect We the People and our Republic. Some of the court and the Chief Justice in particular, have little regard for the American citizen, their employer.

In order to clarify the long winded, rhetorical exchange of dialogue, of which they continued to argue with regards to the Anti- Injunction Act. An inordinate portion of their time arguing whether it was a penalty or tax, subsequently prior to determining which was the appropriate choice, the government withdrew their argument. Now I am obliged to comment on this issue, as this is a prime example of government in action, what fools we mortals be!

The **Anti-Injunction Act**, (chapter. 22 of the Acts for the 2nd United States Congress, 2nd Session, 1 Stat. 333, 28 U.S.C. § 2283), *is a United States federal statute that prohibits any federal court from issuing an injunction against proceedings in any state court, except within three specifically defined exceptions. The Act was enacted on March 2, 1793 as Section 5 of the Judiciary Act of 1793, to alleviate states' fears of federal power.* Take note of their opinion.

*A court of the United States may not grant an injunction to stay proceedings in a state court except as expressly authorized by one, Act of Congress, two where necessary in aid of its jurisdiction, or three to protect or effectuate its judgments.*

*The "tax Anti-Injunction Act" was originally enacted as Pub L. 39-169, 14 Stat.*
*475, section 7421(a) of the Internal Revenue Code of 1954 (now the 1986 Code).*

Though it's a contradiction in terms, Justice Roberts prevailed and the word penalty was injected as he stated *"the word penalty must apply for Constitutional purpose"*. Thus the Chief Justice, has the Supreme court playing with words as if they have no explicit or significance of meaning in his statement *"Though this court will often strain to construe legislation so as to save it against Constitutional attack"*. Think of what Chief Justice John Roberts mind is contemplating, when he stated it must read PENALTY in the Anti-Injunction Act for Constitutional purpose. Then has the gall to suggest, this court will often strain to construe legislation so as to save it against Constitutional attack.

As a citizen I am appalled, outraged and insulted by his interpretations of our Constitution relevant to laws enacted by congresses, to such an extent that one is able to observe his willingness to twist words and case law, in his role as Chief Justice, rather than law needing to align itself with the Constitution, he states the Constitution must align itself with the law. To my view better to my cognizance, I believe he's either totally incompetent, a liar, or probably both.

As I have previously stated, for Justice John Roberts to advocate his ideology and study that any law need not be attacked by our Constitution, again I believe he is a liar and or a fool perhaps both, as I have stated previously. This may have required that he pray to God for mercy.

## Plaintiff's Accusation Charge Two

### Taxing power clause, a mandate of the Affordable Care Act    Chief Justice John Roberts case law, an attempt to support his delusions

Again taking on the words of the court, I have observed in section 5000A(a) the Internal Revenue Service has utilize these words to describe whom they believe comes under the Affordable Care Act…"an applicable  individual", Noah Webster Defines applicable as *an adj. "that which can be applied, or fit to be appropriately applicable".*  Applicable being the mechanism which gives capability for an applicant to apply.   Then again we find Noah Webster defines applicant as: one who applies or makes a request, a petitioner. While individual *as an adj. or noun not divisible, or separable. 2. Existing as separate things, or persons.*

I find the operational use of the word confusing and misperceiving, a simple choice of the word person would have come about suffice. Furthermore, if one is attempting to speak honestly, then they would have used the proper word **applicant,** stating **at** its root purpose.  As in, *I wish to apply for work as a painter, thus becoming an **applicant** by choice.*  Of course this was not their objective, mispresenting the meaning was their intention, their focus.


As for any intent to force an **applicant** when it's clearly a matter of choice is another example of the government's problems with the truth.  Furthermore the issue is beyond and outside the purview and determination of this court.  Below are but a few of Justice Robert's case laws used to support his position.  I have read and copied many other texts of his case law, (available to you upon request) but all are not included in my arguments, as they would not contribute further to the lack of validity to his arguments, nor would enhance mine, only increase the size of the text.

Justice Roberts words "we must if fairly possible" in which he used **Crowell vs. Benson, 285 U.S. 22, 62 (1932)** as an example of his assessment in 5000A IRS 1986 code. Rather this case concerning damages to person operating in U.S. navigable waters, manipulating them to corroborate his contentions. In truth this case was better served under the authority of Admiralty courts, so stated within the body of the transcript.

The following paragraphs of **Crowell vs. Benson 285 U.S.** are but a brief portion of this case, over twenty pages of which I found but one rational reason to further exploit Justice Roberts own position, as the Justice will convolute his own words during the Affordable Care Act case.

The administrative bodies in the cases referred to by the Court, on the contrary, are in no sense fact-gathering **[285 U.S. 22, 89]** or fact-finding tribunals of first instance. They are tribunals of final resort within the scope of their authority. Their concern is with matters ordinarily outside of judicial competence. The deportation of aliens, the enforcement of military discipline, the granting of land patents, and the use of the mails-matters which are within the power of Congress to commit to conclusive executive determination.

Compare Ex parte **Bakelite Corporation, 279 U.S. 438, 451**, 49 S. Ct. 411. Their procedure may be summary and frequently remains. With respect to them, the function of the courts is not one of review but essentially of control-the function of keeping them within their statutory authority. **[285 U.S. 22, 90]** No method of judicial review of the administrative action had been provided by Congress in any of the cases cited; and the question of the power to confine review to the administrative record accordingly did not arise. In each case, the Court held that, if the administrative officer had acted outside his authority, the unwritten law supplied a remedy, and that relief could be had, according to the nature of the case, on bill in equity or habeas corpus. **[285 U.S. 22, 91]**

Without exception I found no reference to the idea of exchanging one word for another, any words, anywhere. As a matter of these issues, the fact stands in these cases is deprived of case law or remedy by federal courts.

The question decided in each case was that Congress should not be taken, in the absence of specific provision, to have intended to subject the person to the uncontrolled action of a public administrative officer. See American School of **Magnetic Healing v. MacNnulty**, 187 <u>U.S. 94, 110</u>, 23 S. Ct. 33. No comparable issue is presented here.

The statement below which is pertinent to this case, was part of the dissenting Justices, Brandeis, Stone and Roberts (not the current Justice Roberts). My evaluation of the affirmative, within the particulars subject to those questions emanating from this case,

I find no suggestion of referring <u>to words not made available, somewhere within the essence, or the body of either of these case.</u>

**Crowell vs Benson**, 285 U. S. 22, 62(1932).
As has been exhibit and explained, **"Every single reasonable construction must be resorted to, in order to save a statue from <u>unconstitutionality</u>"**. The socialist idea is revealed by Justice Roberts attempt at stretching and convoluting these words.

No good reason is suggested why all the evidence which Benson presented to the District Court in this cause could not have been presented before the deputy commissioner; nor why he should have been permitted to try his case provisionally before the administrative tribunal and then to retry it in the District Court upon additional evidence theretofore withheld. To permit him to do so violates the salutary principle that administrative remedied must first be exhausted before resorting to the court, imposes unnecessary and burdensome expense upon the other party and cripples the effective administration of the act. (This is part of the Anti-Injunction Act). Which was settled earlier in The Anti-Injunction Act debacle.

Under the prevailing practice, by which the judicial review has been confined to questions of law, the proceedings before the deputy commissioners [285 U.S. 22, 94] have proved for the most part noncontroversial; and relatively few cases have reached the courts. To permit a contest *de novo (trying a matter anew, as if no decision had been rendered) in the District Court of an issue tried, or tried before the deputy commissioner will, I fear, gravely hamper the effectiveness of the administration of the act itself.*

*The prestige of the deputy commissioner will necessarily be lessened by the opportunity of again litigating facts in the courts. The number of controverted cases may be largely increased. Persistence in controversy will be encouraged, since this idea increases the requirement and of the involvement and interest or activity of upsurge in lawyers. And since the advantage of prolonged litigation lies with the party able to bear heavy expenses, the purpose of the act will be in part defeated. **285 U.S. 22, 95]** In my opinion the judgment of the Circuit Court of Appeal should be reversed and the case remanded to the District Court, sitting as a court of equity, for* consideration and decision upon the record made before the deputy commissioner. Mr. Justice STONE and Mr. Justice ROBERTS join in this opinion.

After having read this case, it was my consensus, it occurred singularly and intended to facilitate another issue entirely, as it had insignificant issue with the question of these words, **penalty** or **taxes.** Nor did there exist any mention of taxes on any issue, or by supplementary means.

Although I did find this relevant decision in the body of "*Crowell vs. Benson*". The contention based upon the judicial power of the United States, as extended 'to all Cases of **Admiralty** *[285 U.S. 22, 49]* and maritime Jurisdiction' (Const. art. 3), presents a distinct question.

In Murray's **Lessee v. Hoboken Land & Improvement Company, 18 How. 272, 284,** this Court, speaking through Justice Curtis, said: *"To avoid misconstruction upon so grave a subject, we think it proper to state that we do not consider congress can either withdraw from judicial cognizance any matter which, from its nature is the subject of a suit at the common law, or in equity, or admiralty. Nor, on the other hand, can it bring under the judicial power a matter which, from its nature, is not a subject for judicial determination".*

**Justice Roberts** in his affirmative decision used Justice Ginsburg statement "The Federal Government does not have the power to order people to buy health insurance.

Section 5000Aa of the Internal Revenue Code "would therefore be unconstitutional if read as a command." Rather Justice Ginsburg misread and misstated when she said, "*Federal Government does have the power to impose a tax on those without health insurance. Section 5000Aa is therefore constitutional, because it can reasonably be read as a tax*". Nowhere is TAX mentioned, as I am sure section 5000Aa is attempting to determine those who, each month shall be required to be covered by minimum essential coverage. Reading on, those failing will be penalized each month. Peculiar that the code reads "*will be penalized each month*", noting the word penalized.

I have judiciously read 5000Aa to the extreme. This section reads… **Requirement** to maintain minimum essential coverage. An applicable individual **shall**…now the words require and shall: **Webster's Require**, "is to ask or insist by right or authority, to order or command." **Shall, "**to be required, in the mandatory sense used in court." Black's Law dictionary, "it means to command" and **require** is used similarly. Please show me where this concept exist in our Constitution, apart from government's duty with respect toward the citizen? The simple fact it simply does not, rather it applies to elected persons to whom serve in any and all political positions.

In this case I came to be obliged to explain the misuse of these two very important words, applicable and individual, now I discover myself in a similar situation, exposing their attempt to confuse the issue with the words, require and shall. However, both these words indicate a command to an **applicant** one having a choice, a simple yea or nay to purchase or not, health care insurance. Please remember this is not about health care, but insurance. I care not how Justice Roberts states or of how **he** thinks it may be similar to, workable or maybe read, but rather what it states in black and white, consistent and appropriately part of the English language. It exist, and is clearly written as a command, unless by chance he is ignorant of the truths, failing our republic's history and the use of the English language. Again we should examine and also consider being enlightened by Thomas Jefferson pertaining to our Constitution related to such a situation, *not to invent against it, conform to the probable one in which it was passed*"

In all six dictionaries I have, three law and three of Webster's dating back to 1828, I find all six state, as to the words require and shall to mean a command. In the face of all these words Chief Justice John Roberts remains akin "the King has no clothes".

**Other cases: Liberty University, Inc. et al v. Geithner et al**
Western District of Virginia **Plaintiffs:**
Liberty University, Inc., and five individuals

**Defendants:**
Timothy Geithner, Kathleen Sibelius, Hilda Solis, Eric Holder

**Judge:**
Norman K. Moon, Referred to: Magistrate Judge Michael F. Urbanski
**Case number:**6:10-cv-00015

**Details:**
Plaintiffs' case is similar to Virginia v. Sibelius, challenging the Patient Protection and Affordable Care Act based on Virginia law. The Plaintiffs object to the use of public funds for abortions, and also raise objections on First Amendment grounds, including an assertion that PPACA expresses a preference for one religion over others. Finally, the Complaint claims that PPACA violates the guarantee of a Republican form of government.

**Status:** An Amended Complaint was filed July 30. The Defendants have filed a Motion to dismiss the case. A hearing on the Motion to Dismiss occurred on October 22. On November 30, the Court granted the Defendants' Motion to Dismiss. On December 1, Plaintiffs filed for appeal.
On May 10, 2011, a three-judge panel from the Fourth Circuit Court of Appeals heard oral arguments in this case. The panel was comprised of two Obama-appointees and one Clinton-appointee. On September 8, 2011, the Fourth Circuit panel dismissed the case. They found that the individual mandate is a tax (the first court to do so), and because of the Anti-Injunction Act, plaintiffs cannot challenge it in court until it is collected (in 2015).
**This case** 3:10-cv-00188-HEH, the state of Virginia is attempting to exercise their right of sovereignty, by way of the ninth and tenth amendments. The court merely brushed it aside. Furthermore, the state of Virginia passed a law protecting its citizens

from monstrous federal action, stating. *"No resident of this Commonwealth, regardless of whether he has or is eligible for* <u>*health insurance coverage*</u> *under any policy or program provided by or through his employer, or a plan sponsored by the Commonwealth or the federal government, shall be required to obtain or maintain a policy of individual insurance coverage. No provision of this title shall render a resident of this Commonwealth liable for any penalty, assessment, fee, or fine as a result of his failure to procure or obtain health insurance coverage."*

"If the citizens of the United States should not be free and happy, the fault will be entirely their own."  George Washington

Again I am persuaded against the Justice stating that *perans patriae,* as We the People rule, hopefully we recuperate our ailing government, is our parental government - supreme.  These Latin words may be found in any law dictionary, but you may already know them.  I found in another court challenging approximately the same action.

**"Liberty University vs. Timothy Geithner, Kathleen Sibelius and Eric Holder".**

In my opinion both of these cases for the  plaintiffs, were wisely presented, nevertheless they were distressingly and  chillingly dismissed   One of the Justices stated the Congress position on the Affordable Care Act by forcing the states to adopt federal standards and mandates, they would forfeit *"<u>or lose their sovereignty</u>"*.  It seems to me either way they have lost, following the <u>command they lose</u>, failing to proceed according to Ninth and Tenth amendments, begets the same loss to the states and their people.  Thus the ninth and tenth amendments are no longer valid, or acknowledged by the national government.  His statement was outrageous and I believe without merit.

This is how Germany began in the early nineteen thirties, the people were beholding to the government, *perans patriae,*  Europe is already well on the road to fascism, tyranny, for their governments no longer are able to grant them the nanny state of which they had become accustom.

**Furthermore Virginia argued; US 213,224,116S, Ct.2106, 2112**

*On the other hand, a penalty imports the notion of a punishment for an unlawful act or omission, "the two words Tax vs. Penalty, are not interchangeable and if exaction is*

*clearly a penalty it cannot be converted into a tax by the simple expedients of calling it such".*

**United States vs. La Franca 282 U.S. 568,51S Ct. 278,280, (1931),** also the Commonwealth points out that elsewhere in the act, Congress specifically described levies as taxes, such as section 9001,9004, 9015, 9017, S. Ct. 449, 450 (1922). To amplify its point, the Commonwealth focuses the Court's attention on a series of cases in which the Supreme Court struck down certain "regulatory taxes" as an unconstitutional encroachment on the State's power of regulation under the Tenth Amendment.

*See Butler, 297 U.S. at 68, 56 S. Ct. at 320. Linder v. United States, 268 U.S. 5, 1718, 45 S. Ct. 446, 449 (1925); Child Labor Tax Case, 259 U.S. at 35, 42 S. Ct. at 451.* In commenting on the limitations on the power of Congress to levy taxes to promote the general welfare, the Court in Butler noted that, *"despite the breadth of the legislative discretion, our duty to hear and to render judgment remains. If the statute plainly violates the stated principle of the Constitution, we must so declare." **Butler, 297 U.S. at 67, 56 S. Ct. at 320; also Kahriger, 345** U.S. at 29, 73 S. Ct. at 513."* Again the commonwealth argued although the Commonwealth concedes that the power of Congress to tax exceeds its ability to regulate under the Commerce Clause, it is not without limitation. *"The law is that Congress can tax under its taxing power that which it can't regulate, but it can't regulate through taxation that which it cannot otherwise regulate." (Tr. 81:18-21, July 1 2010 ) citing.*

**Bailey v Drexel Furniture Co. (Child Labor Tax Case), 259 U.S. 20, 37, 42.**

By comparison, the Commonwealth argues that the Minimum Essential Coverage Provision not only invokes rights reserved to the states, but also seeks to compel activity beyond the reach of Congress. As discussed above, the division of responsibility for regulating insurance between the Commonwealth and the federal government, to the extent relevant, is yet to be adequately staked out in this case. In addition it is my obligation to note in this case, all references to case law, in this particular case by the government are after 1913. In my opinion this fact is so clearly evident and expected, as the income tax law (*the 16Amendment*) plus the Federal Reserve all began in 1913. Think about this incident, chance, I think not, the timing was meant to promote criminal engagement against the people of our republic.

Reading these cases in their entirety, one finds the government in collusion with itself (congress and the courts), as I believe both are without merit on the very face of their arguments. It is my desire to address the constitutional issues involved in the above cases. I am in the status of disbelief as one finds the courts situated between fiction and lies, quite impossible to discover a bit of virtue. This paragraph is my opinion and not necessarily fact, nonetheless I have read and reread using their words to advance my conclusion, these are the Liberty University and Virginia cases.

In a widespread action they merely swept the plaintiffs evidence away, thus deprived of any consideration. In reality they simply destroyed both the 9th and 10th Amendments of our Constitution. Plus among other issues, such as threating to suffer the loss of their soveriegnty.

How can anyone explain the loss of a state's soveriegnty, as each state has their own constitution which demands they remain as sovereign. It's called Judicial Deference and is starved of law, only the dogma of the Justices themselves.

WE WILL ADDRESS SOME OF THE ISSUES IN THE FOLLOWING SECTION BY SHOWING HOW FAR CHIEF JUSTICE JOHN ROBERTS WILL REACH, WITH DECEPTION AND INACCURACIES IN HIS REPRESENTATIONS, IN ORDER TO PROPAGANDIZE HIS AGENDA, JOHN ROBERTS SUGGEST HIS INTERPRETATION FOUND IN THE FOLLOWING SECTIONS OF THE IRS CODE.

U.S. CODE › TITLE 26 › SUBTITLE D › CHAPTER 48 › § 5000A CURRENT THROUGH PUB. L. 114-38. U.S. CODE › TITLE 26 › SUBTITLE D › CHAPTER 48 › § 5000A READS: REQUIREMENT TO MAINTAIN MINIMUM ESSENTIAL COVERAGE, SEE 5000A (A)

## Plaintiff's accusations Charge three

Let us look at 5000A(a) and how it reads: To maintain minimum essential coverage - *An applicable individual shall maintain for each month, beginning after 2013 ensure that the individual, and any dependent of the individual who is an applicable individual, is covered under minimum essential coverage for such.*

I find in Justice Roberts construction of 5000Aa and my analyses of the same, develop an adversarial struggle, John Roberts shapes his attempt by a brazen exploitation of our Constitution and the IRS code. Furthermore, Chief Justice Roberts, implies U.S. Code › Title 26 › Subtitle D › Chapter 48 › § 5000A **(a), A (b), A(c)** one must accept his indulgence in deception as seen here (*if one should reasonably read the section 5000A, then the following sections 5000Aa, Ab and Ac could if reasonably read, as tax*). It appears to me there is not one scintilla of truth in his statement, let's read it again (*if one should reasonably read the section 5000A, then the following sections 5000Aa, Ab and Ac could if reasonably read, as tax*) if one is lacking the ability to read and comprehend English, or he or she require help understanding English, they should acquire help grasping this phrase. These words are interjected by John Roberts and they are never found in 5000A or 5000Aa nor Sec. 5000Ab and 5000Ac as he John Roberts has lied creating the idea they too may be construed to mean tax. I have taken the opportunity and counted the times the word **penalty** is interjected, thus ten times and never once **Tax**. This in the first portion of 5000A, 5000Aa and 5000Ab, (1),(2),(3) 3(a)(b) B and 5000 Ac, all this one half page, the penalty page. If all tax, are as provided for in sec. 8 of Article One of our Constitution, *excises shall be uniform throughout the United States*, how then will it be applied at a sliding scale and fined monthly as detailed in 5000Ac,c)(1thru 3)including sub, sub sections. So like a magician misdirection, now you see it now you are confused with voluminous dissertation, words saying nothing and while examining, but never observing the word tax, finding only penalty.

Reading on to the second page as part of 5000Ac, we observe the scale for which I just mentioned, penalties not taxes outlined on the previous page and all penalties applied as stated. Page 3- 5000Ad gives- explanation to a summary of those who may be exempt, if not excluded by an amendment. These are primarily religious exemptions, under specific situations, nevertheless, Christanty is being brought under attack more so today.

Then fourth page - 5000Ae one finds fourteen sub- and sub-subsections, of which I refrained from lettering. Required contributions, specials rules related to employees, Indexing, Members of Indian Tribes and Tax payers below the taxing threshold plus Hardships. Section 5000Af. Page 5 defines the threshold for minimum coverage. Refraining with regards, alluding to or attempting to explain at this time, all 23 subsections and sub-sub-sections one will encounter. Defining these sections will neither add nor diminish or assist in destroying the individual mandate, check for yourself.


Section 5000Ag page 6 covers "Indoor Tanning Services", while using the word penalty four additional times, while the word tax is non-existent. On page 6 we encounter 5000B, Ba, Bb, Bc, plus as always amendments. This section covers "Elective cosmetic medical procedures." It truly matters not, since 5000Aa was distorted and misrepresented by Justice Roberts. Don't you find it strange as I, we discovered the I.R.S. code covered the entire Affordable Health Care Act in six pages, while Congress required twenty seven hundred plus, aren't we missing something at this point. The full title of this act "Patient Protection and Affordable Care Act and **other things".** Question, what other things? As I read and reread this section of the Affordable Care Act, one will find taxes, regulations, *control by non-elected persons* and therefore highly injurious to this issue, finding these person are not in the medical field and multiple interjections of various types, without answers. Such as this past March 2014, the Obama administration issued its latest "fix" to the troubled roll out of the Affordable Care Act. The Center for Medicare & Medicaid Services issued a guidance that permits federal funds to go to insurers and insureds involved in sale of an individual health insurance outside of either a federally established or state established Exchange. The premise of the guidance is that, in certain states such as Maryland, Massachusetts, Hawaii and Oregon, the complete dysfunctional use of the websites, were intended to determine eligibility for Obamacare subsidies may have led people to enroll in policies off the Exchanges; these purchasers, the guidance directs, those should be treated identically, as if the state Exchanges had made a timely determination and the individuals had enrolled in an Exchange policy.

Further depressing, is the House members and Senators, had never read this 2700 page boondoggle "work of little or no value".  Remember our congresswoman from San Francisco statement, "But we have to pass the bill so you can find out what is in it". Now unfortunately, we have come to discover what's in the bill which Nancy Pelosi insisted we pass so it should become known to all Americans.

Even in a democracy, which we are not, rather sounds quite similar to a dictatorship, certainly not a Republic.

## Plaintiff's Accusation Charge four

While I may address these arguments aggressively, I obtain no comfort of pleasure or exultation in doing so, in fact it grieves me that our government has become corrupt, lazy and incompetent. Of course not all, rather many, example the U.S. Supreme Court of which we are challenging at this time. Again an example, when the court was arguing the Anti-injunction Act, it was determined the word penalty would remain as it was correct and Constitutional, though they argued for some hours, finally Chief Justice John Roberts acknowledged changing penalty to tax would be unconstitutional. Then he simply grabbed a breath and without flinching said (*if one should reasonable read the section 5000A, then the following sections 5000Aa, Ab and Ac could, if reasonably read as tax*). Now we have moved to the subject of the Affordable Care Act from the Anti-Injunction Act. The exchanging of these words have now become constitutional. How?

Justice Roberts … *"The Federal Government does not have the power to order people to buy health insurance. Section 5000A (of THE INTERNAL REVENUE SERVICE) would therefore be unconstitutional if read as a command."* Previously I, due to Webster's definition of the word *"requirement found it to mean a command, especially in the legal utilization, or application, as to insist, a command by authority"*. It appears our Chief Justice is incapable of the meaning of our American English language, as stated earlier. The answer appears in the negative indeed.

Furthermore, he claims magic words or labels should not disable an otherwise Constitutional levy. However he goes on *"the Federal Government does have the power to impose a tax on those without health insurance. Section 5000a is therefore Constitutional because it can be reasonably read as a tax"*. This in his opinion so the question remains where, anywhere has he been given the authority, or granted the power to exchange, convert, or magically insert the word tax in place of the written word Penalty?

In my judgment Justice Roberts not only willingly confers a new definition, (none written), to **requirement**, but insist on our cooperation to presume his argument with Noah Webster's is correct. Furthermore, Justice Roberts comes to the conclusion that penalty and tax are synonymous words, since they are synonymous therefore could be read as being the same, thus we must assume he maintains the mantel of Chief Justice, ultimate authority and critic of the American English dictionary plus Black's Law Dictionary.

Again we find Black's law definition *"The rule by which an instrument will be governed",* whereupon the substance of my argument on this subject rest. Since Justice Roberts ruled it unconstitutional if read as a command, that being said it is a command, as a consequence, therefore unconstitutional, ah. Surprise, here comes a second decision by Justice Roberts in order to satisfy the socialist in our republic.

Hence asserting his position from the same Internal Revenue Service code 5000Aa *minimum essential coverage* is therefore constitutional, because it can be reasonably read as a tax, WHAT!

Please allow me to read section 5000A of the I.R.S. code. *"Requirement (command) to maintain"* that's all no more no less, concluded. *Then the following sections 5000Aa, Ab and Ac could if reasonably read as tax)* nether the word tax or penalty are to be found in sec.5000Aa, although in 5000Ab , 5000Ac of I.R.S. one will find the word penalty on ten occasions but never once tax.

In the interest of untangling these atrocities, let's conjure up an idea following Justice Robert's line of thinking. As we move in his direction we find, *"the idea of taxes acceptable, with regards to the Affordable Care act and this mandate of a tax to punish those who fail to implement the requirement, maintaining minimum essential coverage".*

In doing so, I find in our Constitution that excise taxes must be uniform across our republic, the question seems to me, is Justice Roberts saying that all citizens involved with the Affordable Care Act must pay a uniform excise. The Constitution is very clear on this significant subject, Article one, section eight, first paragraph, ***imposts and excises shall be uniform throughout the United States*** All taxes except imposts and income tax are excise.

Thus to tax some citizens without taxing all others at the same rate would be unconstitutional. However, if he's suggesting the tax is set upon one select group for failing to comply with a required minimum essential insurance coverage, (their words) straight away that's an entirely new question to be considered.

If in fact that select group is in truth punished for failure to comply, (taxed per John Roberts) then failing to comply has developed into a command, come about by fear of retribution. I am unaware of the ability for the United States Government to coerce anyone or any group by threat of force to comply with their wishes except by penalty. However, John Roberts notion this act may be enforced by its open ended stipulation of coercion, thus it remains unconstitutional on the face of "stipulation of coercion".

Then if a person or groups of persons do in fact comply, their freedom of choice has been converted into an ineffectual statement, annulled and void. Which shall it be Justice Roberts, one or the other not both, shall the Constitution rule or you sir.

*Those, then, who controvert the principle that the Constitution is to be considered in court as a paramount law are reduced to the necessity of maintaining that courts must close their eyes on the Constitution, and see only the law, the statute or treaty. "This doctrine would subvert the very foundation of all written constitutions" Justice Marshal 1803*

After this time, 1803 the courts chose to operate using a tactic called Judicial Deference and upon this ideology they became situated to support or defeat the laws by their reading and choosing and by obligatory events, create new laws. Their interpretation of the laws of congress deprived of the influence and authority of our Constitution, gives them crucial choice. Acting upon this idea is unconstitutional.

However, let's go back to where I deviated momentarily, next section 5000Ac called "AMOUNT OF PENALTY" c1, a &b c2 a- … on to the next page, four more times I find the word penalty, and how the penalty will be inflicted and how one will be penalized. Their scale for exaction (extortion) for the applicable individual,

74

supposedly we have the **mandate**. Thus Democrats, like Nancy Pelosi House Speaker and Harry Reid leader of the Senate, demanded of their fellow members, sponsorship. Note: Now an *Applicable Individual* received an additional title, **taxpayer**, under certain conditions in sec.5000Ac, strange how they slink in and changed one's title from "applicable individual", to "taxpayer", how did that happen?  The vote was 220215, all 171 Republicans and 34 Democrats dissented.

Therefore, most of **we the people** possibly believed the Supreme Court generally represented conservative views, instead led by Chief Justice Roberts, with four other Justices, Ginsburg, Sotomayor, Breyer, and Kagan, all socialist, thus the Affordable Care Act became law.  Acting correctly upon the socialistic ideology and with full intent of supporting the act "Patient Protection and Affordable Care Act and other things".  With deep loathing for our Constitution, not without additional "socialism plus" also coming from the President. In true rumination, nothing could possibly be closer to the truth, if it weren't so brutal, it would be a practical joke, a hoax, placed upon our republic, the act is at best a nonentity in value, completed with total deception.  If all this sounds as if I'm mangling the ideology of Justice Roberts, it's because I am attacking his line of deception with regards to this particular case and in my opinion a liar, therefore I believe it has not one scintilla of merit. As a result, with consideration to the *Affordable Care Act and other things,* this case is a study in fraud, based upon the Internal

Revenue Service Code, punishing those whom chose not to be converted into "an *applicable individual, or a mandate for minimum essential coverage*".

Thus by means of coercion, one is commanded to take part in a government program, never knowing the results.  As the name suggest, "Patient Protection Affordable Care Act **and other things**".  Over time I have read most of the Affordable Act and Other Things. We are now beginning to grasp the meaning of Other Things. This is pure and simple fraud commited by those who chose to serve, in essence a mafia style operation, run by the national government's Gestapos.

Affordable Act and Other Things. We are now beginning to grasp the meaning of Other Things. This is pure and simple fraud commited by those who chose to serve, in essence a mafia style operation, run by the national government's Gestapos.

While on the subject of fraud, again let's go back in history. The era, the great depression less than three out of four workers were earning a few bits of money, others walking the streets, families in soup lines. Sound similar to anything parallel to today...yes you bet. The Congress along with Pres. Roosevelt brought into law Social Security, Workmen's comp. Unemployment Compensation, Old age insurance, etc., All were established as national insurance programs based on actuarial principles, nationally administered and financed entirely by taxes on employers and employees. It has become an inseparable part of our way of life, Social Security is here to stay. All this was accomplished through a coordinated effort performed by our Congress, Administration and Courts, then called the "New Deal". All this ensued amid a massive depression, nothing but a massive Hoax, controlled by the national government but implemented by the states. Again my opinion, Christian people failed and government moved in and today those programs are failing agendas, bordering on all programs.

I am confident of my opinion, there are only three probable consequences for one to describe from Justice Robert's decision, with respect to the individual mandate of the Affordable Health Care Act. One: to establish socialism for the politico. Two: an act of total ignorance and arrogance toward our unalienable rights given by God, Three: a pure act of dishonesty. Moreover, John Roberts is so erratically confused regarding the issue of law and statute, his belief *"is to protect by whatever method deemed necessary, to keep the law or statue from attack from all possible objections, and furthermore to protect it from an attack by the Constitution"* these are his words. This man Justice Roberts through his own words, illustrates his plans are as faulty as much his ideology, and an abundant supply and source of socialist dogma from Barack Obama. I certainly am opposed to this exercise of thought, and I strongly accept the idea that our Constitution is the true law of our republic,

*The Supreme law being a form which all other laws are guided and obliged to align themselves.* Again the words of Justice Marshal "*I ask if this isn't true then what's the purpose of a constitution, any constitution"?*

Yet again I am obliged to inform Justice Roberts he is mistaken, in fact a Constitution is the established structure or the form a republic state or nation declares, it is which determines if law is true law. Therefore, in our republic all laws are written by the House of Representatives and Senate therefore all laws are essentially compelled to pass the framework of our Constitution, thus this concept gives meaning to our court system, local, state and national. Passing laws willy-nilly would lead to unscrupulous corruption, yet nothing beyond anything that is confronting us today. In truth, rather not reality of laws passed currently, as few are established from the Constitution, which is the limit or scope of a statute thereof.

So please Justice Roberts, at a bare minimum, read and study our Founding Fathers, in basic terms learn the meaning and try to appreciate while getting the embodiment of our Constitution. I continue to stress this issue, due to what I see as the importance of its meaning and the very core of our republic's existence.

### Chief Justice Marshall in Marbury vs. Madison (1803)

> "It is emphatically the province and duty of the Judicial Department [the judicial branch] to say what the law is. Those who apply the rule to particular cases must, of necessity, expound and interpret that rule. If two laws conflict with each other, the Courts must decide on the operation of each.
> So, if a law [e.g., a statute or treaty] be in opposition to the Constitution, if both the law and the Constitution apply to a particular case, so that the Court must either decide that case conformably to the law, disregarding the Constitution, or conformably to the Constitution, disregarding the law, the Court must determine which of these conflicting rules governs the case. This is of the very essence of judicial duty. If, then, the Courts are to regard the Constitution, and the Constitution is superior to any ordinary act of the Legislature, the Constitution, and not such ordinary act, must govern the case to which they both apply.

Those who controvert the doctrine of our Constitution, as a consequence to be considered in court as the paramount law, therefore reduced the Constitution to the inevitability of maintaining the courts ideology. Consequently the court closes their eyes, no longer seeing the Constitution, rather see only the law [e.g., the statute or treaty].

Which of course is not the opinions or actual positions designed by the framers of our skillfully complete, however remarkable their work, the description and meaning persists and remain quite clear. Today the courts policy would subvert the very foundation of all written Constitutions.

I totally believe the concept of the Constitution's preeminence, whenever, wherever or however the legislators create a law, then the law must meet the purview of the Constitution. Thus the use of such a simplistic idea and is only confusing when it is twisted by those wanting to mutilate and deface its meaning. Please remember the ideology of Thomas Jefferson, *we were endowed by our creator with certain unalienable rights, among them Life, Liberty and the pursuit of happiness, government are instituted among men deriving their just power from the consent of the governed.* Never an idea of having a legislative body to whom we are answerable, or them to themselves singularly, while the courts were only inspired by their own thoughts, thus the law would emerge many times from their meager judgmental ideas, merely as prattling's, this without our Constitution to guide them.

This without a Bible, a guidebook for all persons which no written ideology should dominate, all other laws regardless from whence they may have taken place, or the issues may well entail. If this were the progression for congressional law being approved by the courts, then there's no need for a Constitution, but one is there and needed, both the Bible and our Constitution are there for all to read and comprehend.

This is the mere purpose of our Constitution, while maintaining a check on Congress and the Executive Branch, separate but equal entities at all times. Thus our Constitution is a wall between government and We the People. Then we find the Bill of Rights, the first Ten Amendments in the Constitution, due to the drafters hindsight, knew their exclusion of certain personal rights would be deficient, never to be permitted by all states, as they were soveriegn.

For decades now the courts at all levels have created law by their decisions, this concept, this objective is to rule our republic from the courtroom. Consequently, in conjunction with a president encompassing all the attributes of a king, nevertheless, a prodigy of the courts, all this and no mention of God Almighty, how far we have fallen since the inception and embodiment of our Constitution.

Accordingly, this is why I have considered it the failure of Christians to press our congress, administration and courts to do the work they chose, then elected to serve and execute. I'm well aware and appreciate the fact some Christians and Christian groups are genuinely involved, first in spreading the Gospel of our Lord God and Jesus Christ, then are persistent on influencing the government to think of God in an acquiescent temperament. Hence, following good judgment, essences for intellectual reason and significance of actions by men who, with God's wisdom and help, created our Constitution and this imposing Christian republic.

It's my opinion the courts, in particular the Supreme Court is beyond basic accepted thinking, shallow, they deem the Constitution be rewritten, by them. How gross my disgust and aversion has me bewildered, consequently our need for moving on is a humbling notion.

## Plaintiff's Accusation Charge five

In this section I will attempt to further the argument for an analysis of case law as used by all federal courts, including of the U.S. Supreme court. After reading several with regards to the issue at hand, I became aware of their rationalization. Exercising this approach rather than a direct interpretation of the Constitution, they practice the convolution of words, slither between other court decisions, not necessarily near or similar to the subject in question.

I would accept this premise, if the solitary objective were to facilitate their application of the Constitution. In my opinion, not to construct an entirely new scheme able to forfeit those laws and philosophies of our republic's Constitution. As I am firmly convinced our Constitution unquestionably means today, as the day it was written. It was not in the heart of those wise and brave men, inspired by God to imagine otherwise. Only foolish men attempt to controvert and change meanings to fit their entangled judgments.

For myself, the meaning is quite clear in **Gibbons vs. Ogden** (1822) 22 U.S.1 a case Justice Roberts strolls out, but seems unable to clearly figure out or comprehend its meaning.

**Gibbons vs. Ogden**     More of Justice Robert's case law.

> *"If, as always has been understood, the sovereignty of Congress, <u>though limited to specified objects, is plenary as to those objects</u>, the power over commerce with foreign nations and among the several states is vested in Congress as absolutely as it would be in a single government, having in its Constitution <u>the same restrictions on the exercise of the power as are found in the Constitution of the United States.</u>"*

I discover nowhere the suggestion to change words or meaning of the written Constitution, or for integrating any other significance or connotations as to the statements rendered earlier by Justice Marshall.

In addition case law was not a practice in the early eighteen hundreds, the Constitution being the base line used in the determination of their decisions, why the courts strayed is open to question.

**U.S. vs. Halper 490 U.S. 435**    Justice Robert's case law.

*Relying primarily on United States v. Halper, 490 U. S. 435 (1989), the Bankruptcy Court decided that the assessment constituted a form of double jeopardy. The court rejected the <u>State's argument</u> **that the tax was not a penalty** because it was designed to recover law_enforcement costs; as the court noted, the DOR "failed to introduce one scintilla of evidence as to cost of the above government programs or costs of law enforcement incurred to combat illegal drugs.*

This case was about taxes and double jeopardy, nowhere within the disposition of the case were there considerations for the meaning of, words or alterations of the same. The courts determination it was a penalty thus not a tax.

**Kurth Ranch 511 U.S.**    Justice Robert's case law

*A legislature's description of a statute as civil does not foreclose the possibility that it has a punitive character, and that a defendant convicted and punished for an offense may not have a non- remedial civil penalty imposed against him for the same offense in a separate proceeding, the Court did not consider whether a tax may similarly be characterized as punitive. However, the Court's recognition that the extension <u>of a</u> <u>**socalled tax penalizing feature can cause it to lose it's character as such and**</u> <u>**become a mere penalty**</u>.*

This case is solely on the subject of taxes, taxes levied by the state of Montana. Again no argument or discussion of altering the meaning of words because Justice Roberts seems to believe penalty is simply the same as tax, were not an issue in this case.

I have read several cases in this regard, some used by Justice Roberts but was unable to find where the word penalty and tax are synonymous, in fact never appeared in the same paragraph, subsequently, whichever these Justices are ignorant of the use of these words or just exploited their meaning.

Never citing or applying the Constitution other than the Congress use of the taxing clause. On the other hand the use of an application of the law itself was never argued or objections confronted by this panel of Supreme Court Justices in the argument over

Affordable Care Act. This case, Kurth Ranch 511 U.S. existed concerning growing marijuana in the state of Montana. Ultimately the owner of the ranch was fined (penalized) per pound of the illegal plant. There never was an issue of word changing or synonymous meaning. Justice Roberts's case is without merit and on its very face must be recognized as such, this case totally inerrant to Justice John Roberts use as an issue, unquestionably outside of the " Kurth Ranch 511 U.S." case.

**Parsons vs. Bedford- 28 U.S. 448. case of 1830**

*If, indeed, the construction contended for at the bar were to be given to the act of Congress, we entertain the most serious doubts whether it would not be unconstitutional. No court ought, unless the terms of an act rendered it unavoidable, to give a construction to it which should involve a violation, however unintentional, of the Constitution. The terms of the present act may well be satisfied by limiting its operation to modes of practice and proceeding in the court below without changing the effect or conclusiveness of the verdict of the jury upon the facts litigated at the trial.*

This is simply a portion of this case, moreover for that reason, I could find nothing to support Justice Roberts own opinions, while taking into account the Affordable Care Act. However it began and is a common law case.

## HOOPER v. PEOPLE OF STATE OF CALIFORNIA, 155 U.S. 648 (1895)

**HOOPER**
**v.**

**PEOPLE OF STATE OF CALIFORNIA.**
**No. 7.**
**January 7, 1895**

**Section 623 of the Political Code of the state of California provides as follows:**

*The insurance commissioner must require every company, association, or individual not incorporated under the laws of this state and proposing to transact insurance business by agent or agents in this state, before commencing such business to file in his office a bond to be signed by the person or firm, officer or agent, as principal, with two sureties to be approved by the commissioner, in the* *penal sum of $2,000 for each insurance company, association, firm or individual for whose account it is proposed to collect premiums of insurance in this state.* 'The condition of such bond to be as follows: *First. That the person or firm, agent or officer named therein, acting on behalf of the company, association, firm or individual, named therein, will pay to the treasurer of the county, or city and county in which the principal office of the agency is located, such sum per quarter, quarterly in advance, for a license to transact an insurance business or such other license [155 U.S. 648, 649] as may be imposed by law as long as the agency remains in the hands of the person or firm, agent or officer named as principal in the bond.*

*Second. That the person or firm, officer or agent will pay to the state all stamp or other duties on the gross amounts insured inclusive of renewals on existing policies.*

*Third. That the person, firm, agent or corporation named therein will conform to all provisions of the revenue or other laws made to govern them.*'

While reading the above, one readily discovers this case refers to insurance and how it need be applied in the state of California, the agents and or firm representing a company association, etc. etc.

None of the above cases have any resemblance to the case of which we are concerned, the above case never presents any lawyers or Justices as referring in any way to taxes, although a few instances are made regarding penalties, only in relationship to the penal code, with the possibility of being guilty of misdemeanor.

This case was eighteen plus pages long and has no influence what so ever regarding the Affordable Care Act, nor does it as Justice Roberts suggest, the government asked to interpret the case ( Hooper vs. state of California) as a mandate to tax, if it would otherwise violate the Constitution. Granting the Act the full measure of deference owed to federal statues, it can be so read, for the reasons set forth below. Please remember this California case was tried in California.

Does he assume we are all fools, I have with others read this case Hooper vs. California three times, nowhere does the government request we frame this case as to read it as a mandate imposing a tax, the word "tax" would never even fit this case which as I stated and one can read for themselves, it is about insurance, agents, firms, companies which involves insurance for large ships, etc., etc. with regards to California state law.

I am irritated, more to the point infuriated when he reaches so far, leading one to momentarily question their own reliability to the proceedings.

Again I am of the opinion Justice Roberts continues to reach in the extreme in order to support his ridiculous ideology, attempting to avoid the truth, using case law, rather than first an application of our Constitution. Reading Justice Roberts decision directly from the transcripts, one detects a feeling of desperation coming from his quoting case law to the extreme, grasping at straws, reminiscent of Don Quixote chasing his windmills, at any rate, is Justice Roberts in anyway "the man of La Mancha". The case directly above has no value in our situation regarding the Affordable Care Act, there is no merit on its face fitting to support John Roberts contentions. Of course his ideology is in opposition to many of his other decisions, lacking surprise?

### United States vs. Reorganized & Fabricators 95-325

*The District Court and the Tenth Circuit affirmed.   Held: 1. The "tax" under § 4971 (a) was not entitled to seventh priority as an "excise tax" under § 507(a)(7)(E), but instead is, for bankruptcy purposes, a penalty to be dealt with as an ordinary, unsecured claim. Pp. 218-226.*

*Congress included no such reference in §507(a)(7)(E), even though the bankruptcy code.   Code provides no definition of "excise," "tax," or "excise tax." This absence of any explicit connection between §§ 507(a)(7)(E) and 4971 is all the more revealing in light of this Court's history of interpretive practice in determining whether a "tax" so called in the statute creating it is also a "tax" for its purpose.*

*The Court's cases in this area looks to whether the purpose of an exaction is support of the government or punishment for an unlawful act. If the concept of a penalty means anything, it means punishment for an unlawful act or omission. That is what*

84

*this exaction is. The § 4971 exaction is imposed for violating a separate federal statute requiring the funding of pension plans, and thus has an obviously penal character. Pp. 224-225. The complaint, judgment was entered for the company against the collector for the full amount, with interest. The writ of error is prosecuted by the collector direct from the District Court under section 238 of the Judicial Code (Comp. St. 1215).... and later approved a reorganization plan for CF&I giving lowest priority (and no money) to claims for non-compensatory* <u>penalties</u>*.*

There are twenty pages presented for the decision of this case, again I could not find within the resolution of the court, anywhere stated they could justify the use of twisting words by the court to correspond with the intent of the law, presented by Congress. The facts of this case were argued on the merits of excise taxes and state rights, the Ninth and Tenth amendments primarily. This case decided three points. **One**, the IRS was not within the essence of its authority, **two**, the congress had improperly exercised its agenda in this case, **three**, the case should have been under the jurisdiction of state laws in accordance with the Constitution at the Tenth amendment, the sovereignty of the state and its people.

### U.S. Supreme BAILEY v. DREXEL FURNITURE CO., 259 U.S. 20 (1922)

**BAILEY**

v.

**DREXEL FURNITURE CO.**
**CHILD LABOR TAX CASE.**
**No. 657.**

**Argued March 8, 1922.**
**Decided May 15, 1922.**
[259 U.S. 20, 21] Mr. Solicitor General Beck, of Washington D. C., for plaintiff in error.
[259 U.S. 20, 28] Mr. Wm. P. Bynum, of Greensboro, N. C., for defendant in error.
[259 U.S. 20, 34]

*Mr. Chief Justice TAFT delivered the opinion of the Court.*

*This case presents the question of the constitutional validity of the Child Labor Tax Law. The plaintiff below, the Drexel Furniture Company, is engaged in the manufacture of furniture in the Western district of North Carolina. On September 20, 1921, it received a notice from Bailey, United States collector of internal revenue for the district and that it had been assessed $6,312.79 for having during the taxable year 1919 employed and permitted to work in its factory a boy under 14 years of age, thus incurring the tax of 10 per cent. on its net profits for that year. The company paid the tax under protest, and, after rejection of its claim for a refund, brought this suit. On demurrer to an amended complaint, judgment was entered for the company against the collector for the full amount, with interest. The writ of error is prosecuted by the collector direct from the District Court under section 238 of the Judicial Code (Comp. St. 1215*

I conclude from this case the IRS attempted in error to collect a tax, instead of the government charging Drexel Furniture in the question of validity with regards in their action with the "child labor tax law". I identified no questions concerning an issue of taxes other than the IRS mistakenly collecting a tax illegally and a penalty was never in question.

Thus as for our purpose, the issue with regards to this case is lacking support or merit.

## Plaintiff's Accusation Charge six

Additionally and must be seen as foremost, the National Government's power is limited by our Constitution, Bill of Rights, especially concerning the Ninth and Tenth Amendments regarding those stating the sovereignty of all states and its people are supreme. In fact the National government must adhere to all of the amendments in our Bill of Rights. Where in the Constitution has the National Government been given the power to control the choice of the people, or it's state and people forced into purchasing **anything**, let alone insurance to cover one's own health.

I have faith in the American people to deem what is best for themselves and their families, not some outrageous political hacks in Washington D.C. I challenge any politician to confront and deny this statement, especially, Nancy Pelosi, Harry Reid and President Obama, who knows now we have only fifty states not fifty seven. Justice Roberts, what you are looking for **just does not exist.** Regardless, if I or any person or persons had the opportunity to challenge these cases or others like them, they would only lie, more smoke and mirrors or act as if we aren't capable of comprehending the entire picture simultaneously. Let me read you from *The Fifth Amendment, section four, "nor be deprived of Life Liberty or property, without due process of law"*.

The affordable Care Act deprives us these God given rights. Plus the entire Seventh Amendment. Mr. Noah Webster *"In United States the unwritten law, the law that receives its binding force from time long-established usage and universal reception, all come from God, in distinction from the written law or statute."*

One could go on endlessly with this ill-advised activity, but to what end. The point of case law, actually accomplished by staffers, is meant to help with their opinion regarding the subject's substance. The fact we have a Constitution is secondary at best, in spite of this We the People move on aimlessly, accepting our loss of freedoms as if there is no recourse. While scores of unaware persons are unacquainted of the facts, nor knowledge of these facts are realized, save for a small number. In our

Constitution and its great predecessor the Declaration of Independence, without which there would be no Constitution, in my opinion accomplished by an undersized number of honest and wise men, supported by God, giving us a Constitution unlike any other. There are but few recognizing all our freedoms come from God, governments simply embezzles and acquires by default our liberty doing so in a humungous method. Words possessed absolute significance during the writing of the U.S. Constitution. I am of the conviction it **was** these rights' where Justice Roberts avoids the truth, or persist in acting merely dismissive of the truth.

Ben Franklin, when asked with respect to what the convention was about " *a Constitution if you will keep it"* I ask, how could we have gotten so far from God and country.

I've gotten off the point, back to Justice Roberts and the other Justices, Ginsburg, Breyer, Sotomayor and Kagan never having adjudicated a case, till being appointed to the Supreme Court in 2009 as they are presently our concern. Justice Roberts stated that the shared responsibility payments are not a penalty but a tax. Then he, Justice Roberts argued in the Anti-Injunction Act with regards to the Affordable Care Act it was a penalty not a tax appointed by the Constitution.

Visit Section 5000A (b). To the extent Justice Roberts manipulates the meaning of this section and that according to this section creates a mandate, thus establishing a condition while not owning health insurance will trigger a tax, the required payment headed for the IRS. Under that theory, the mandate is not a legal command to buy insurance, rather, it makes going without insurance just another thing the government taxes, like buying gasoline, taxed, or purchasing tobacco, taxed which you purchase by choice and pay the tax, by choice. And if the mandate is in effect just like a tax on certain taxpayers who do not purchase health insurance, those who chose not to buy it are without insurance, like those who made the other choices. The question is not whether that is the most natural interpretation of the mandate, as it is, but only whether it is a "deceitfully possible" one.

The question is not a matter of mandate (command) as the government cannot command you to do nothing whatever, unless in the service of the military when in actual service in time of war or public danger.

Otherwise, as to the point Justice Scalia said "if so they could force you to eat broccoli" guessing he is not a broccoli fan, I love that assertion.

I find We the People, are so anemic and pathetic to locate persons capable of serving in our government who are devoid of corruption and truly willing to serve. Are they not to be found?

**Crowell v Benson, 285 U.S. 2, 62 (1932)."**

Returning to the words of one Chief Justice John Roberts, "if read reasonably it could fairly possible read tax". Of course this is not the most reasonable, his own words, and furthermore it is only "fairly possible". Nowhere in the case, Crowell v Benson does it suggest, in any way that one can read the meaning of any word essential to the case into whatever one wishes to twist its meaning. Furthermore, in Crowell v Benson does it suggest that any essential word or words, where one argues what is natural and another possible exist as one together. However, the words "most natural", and whether it is "fairly possible" are not the same as the actual word. As penalty, which is the word written in 5000 A(b) and tax being imaginative. The words penalty and tax have entirely different meanings, one, penalty is defined for doing something wrong while taxes are established through Article One sec. 8 and its enumerated topics, sadly many other schemes to deprive the people of their hard work, only to create programs undesirable to the majority of the folks.


Then Justice Roberts stated the issue in the Affordable Care Act is the same as the cigarettes tax which is used as revenue as well as a preventive issue. Now Justice Roberts declares the government profits from these taxes but also to thwart smoking to some degree. The habit of smoking is a matter of choice, of which the impediment of smoking may result to some degree. The desire of smoking is a matter of choice, of which one knowingly choses to pay the taxes and smoke, as I have enumerated

89

previously. Where is the law, in 5000A, 5000Aa, 5000Ab and 5000Ac, nor is it anywhere. There are no such national laws preventing one from smoking, thus there is no penalty attached for doing what one wishes, only the attached tax which the person choses to pay by their choice for smoking.

Again he addresses taxes, simply in a direct manner, as he has chosen to elect gasoline as a tax paid without choice if one wishes to purchase fuel. At the pump one makes a conscious choice, no law to ponder, merely shall I bring into being a purchase? Once I choose to purchase fuel I agree to pay the tax, no influence by government, no penalty, just the need for fuel, or buy a bicycle.

I am a simple man making simple decisions, customarily to see truth through our God given Rights, not though volumes of useless words contained in buildings, contrived by incompetent, bungling party persons. Likewise, Justice Roberts attempts an analogy of cigarettes and gasoline with the Affordable Care Act, where I make a distinction, a competent comparison, Justice John Roberts remarks were simply injudicious comments, adding nothing to the issue at hand.

I believe the Affordable Care Act to be as Senator DeMint states *"violates beyond the rule of law"*. We find on page 1001 of the act *"reduce the per capita rate of growth"* raise revenues on Medicare beneficiary premiums under section 1818, 1818a, or 1839 sounding as if their idea of not rationing is a lie, seems to me as if they simply never had any intention to pay, long or short term.

If one cares with regards to these particular issues read pages 1004, 1011, 1017, 1019, 1020 and I found the reading of 1019 analysis for myself is: these unelected engineers of our lives have instituted a law, exclusive of any directive from the Senate or the House that would have any recourse to this Section of the bill, that would change the recommendations of the board (politico) of non- elected persons.

This section 1020 states to my satisfaction that if congress may find something to become distressed and affronted regarding these foregoing sections, it may over rule by bringing to a vote of three-fifths of the House.

Image an unelected body of persons instructing our congress what to perform, or possibly act negatively upon our Constitution.

The origin for Justice Roberts' argument is in Article One, Section 8 first clause: "*the congress shall have the power to lay and collect taxes*". These powers are limited to those enumerated. Again Justice Roberts, as many others have misused the general welfare section. Noah Webster a brilliant man, composing a dictionary defining the meaning of the words at the turn of the century, being the early 1800's, for us to examine in order to better appreciate those words, as meant when the Constitution was written.

The word welfare used in the above section meant, "*An exception from misfortune, sickness, calamity or evil; the enjoyment of health and the common blessings of life, prosperity and happiness*". One must ask, is this in alignment with Justice Roberts objective for his argument, to facilitate the meaning of Article One sec. 8, first clause. If so, then the ability to tax all things, all people and freedoms is pure fascist besides socialism. Then again I accuse Justice Roberts of ignorance and or deceit or both.

Justice Roberts, your decision is established upon corruption, specifically fabrication, mendacity and duplicity pandering to the politico.

Again we must go deeper into the erroneous ideology of both Justice Ginsburg and Roberts. Their entanglement of a piece of our Constitution is unique if not so constantly inaccurate, designated "the necessary and proper clause". These enumerated powers grants congress to "*make all laws which shall be necessary and proper for carrying into execution the foregoing powers, and all other powers vested by the constitution in the Government of the United States, or in any department or officer thereof.*" This clause as stated "foregoing powers" is in reference to the immediate paragraph preceding this clause. That paragraph is "*the ten square miles and all determined buildings within, and called the seat of the Government of the U.S. and to exercise Authority over all places purchased by the consent of the legislature… and to make all laws which shall be necessary and proper for carrying into execution the **forgoing powers**… Article one sec. 8 clause 16.* Mr. Noah Webster indication of "foregoing" to mean, "Proceeding, going before in time or place, as a foregoing clause in a writing, antecedent."

The fundamentals in the issues presented, emanates from honest study of the facts, Justice Roberts arguments exhibited a convoluted mindset, constantly attempting to change the meaning of his own use of case law. Altering the meaning of simple words to fit his agenda, misuse of the Constitution with the intent of having it match his needs. When one considers his arguments, Justice Roberts himself, destroyed his own endeavors. The compelling magnitude of evidence presented by necessity, simply designed and required for the conviction of Justice Roberts, for supporting the objective of destroying our health care and insurance plans. Thus we as a people are obliged to overturn these fallacious actions and commence with impeachment proceedings against the Justice, for high crimes in opposition to an effective economy, choice and liberty for We the People.

**In summary** First fact: An applicable individual being a person applying for a position and as such, remains a person merely applying **by choice**.

Second fact: "Shall, as well as require, is a command given by authority", Noah Webster *"to demand as by right or authority"*.

Third Fact: Penalty and taxes, Noah Webster, "penalty*",* by law or judicial authority *for the commission of a crime"*, taxes, *"to lay and collect taxes, impost and excises"* or assess upon citizens to defray the expense of government. Article one, section 8, clause 1, U.S. Constitution.

Fourth fact: Synonyms, *"A name or word having the same significance as another"*, again Noah Webster. The idea of two words of the same significance creating a synonym, is a common way to articulate ones speech.

Fifth fact: Case law, a method of supporting an idea or thought lawyers and Jurist will use, seeking previous laws to assistant and or support their overview of a particular disposition or agenda.

Sixth fact. Convolution, the twisting or winding of words into something the words were never intended to indicate or suggest.

92

# Part Two Plus

### Does the Declaration of Independence Still Matter?

Our Declaration of Independence was an intentional list of grievances against a degenerate monarch, both King George III and the colonists who disagreed with his rule are long dead. The ideology promoted by Samuel Adams and written primarily by Thomas Jefferson, to the cause which led to this declaration, it read in part, *"If ye love wealth better than liberty, the tranquility of servitude than the animating contest of freedom, go from us in peace. We ask not your counsels or arms. Crouch down and lick the hands which feed you. May your chains sit lightly upon you, and may posterity forget that ye were our countrymen".*

Still many exist today, countless of those people who continue to argue that the Declaration is obsolete. In fact, this is exactly what those who called themselves "progressives" were saying more than a century ago. Woodrow Wilson, one of the most infamous early progressives, argued during the 1912 presidential campaign that all that Progressives ask or desire is for *"permission...to interpret the Constitution according to the Darwinian principle,"* meaning that it should promote an ever expanding set of powers for an ever-expanding government and atheistic in principle. The problem he declared, was that pesky Declaration of Independence.

An array of citizens from our republic have never gotten beyond *Life, Liberty and the Pursuit of Happiness* from within the Declaration of Independence. The certainty of a fixed point in time, our Declaration of Independence was meant to be static, fixed and constant. As the statements in this document remains the same today, especially with the facts, viewing the considerations of our current plight.

But in fact the Declaration is more than a litany of complaints. Its greater meaning is a statement of the conditions of legitimate political authority and the proper ends of government. It proclaimed that political rule would, from then on, reside in the sovereignty of the people. *"If the American Revolution had produced nothing but the Declaration of Independence,"* wrote the great historian Samuel Eliot Morrison, *"it would have been worthwhile."*

The ringing phrases of the document's famous second paragraph are a powerful synthesis of American constitutional and republican government theories. All men have a right to liberty as they are by nature equal, which is to say none are inherently superior and deserve to rule, or are inferior and deserve to be ruled.

Therefore, all are endowed with all these rights from God, the rights are unalienable, which means that they cannot be given up or taken away. And because sovereign people equally possess these rights, governments derive their just powers from the consent of those they govern. Government's purpose is to secure these fundamental rights, God given and although caution tells us that governments should not be changed for frivolous reasons. However, the people maintain the right to revise or abolish government when it becomes devastating to those ideas and now asserting Thomas Jefferson words, *"to institute new government laying it's foundation on such principles and organizing it's powers in such form, as to them shall seem most likely to affect their safety and happiness."*

The Declaration also insists we have the right to "the pursuit of happiness." A higher component of that pursuit, of course, is being able to worship as we please. This right is our fundamental religious liberty. Yet that right seems to be under attack today by our government alongside many others. When will American people be willing to defend that right, our God given rights and repair our republic to its authentic and accurate beginnings, a people believing with an objective of *"a people who are called by my name, will humble themselves and pray and seek my face and turn from their wicked ways, then will I hear from heaven and will forgive their sin and will heal their land"* 2nd Chronicles (7:14)

I firmly believe that George Washington's faith in God, made him the absolute and utterly complete General, leading a small band of non-professional soldiers to thwart the most powerful military force at that time. Furthermore, his presidency was without a doubt one of the finest we as a people have ever possessed and honored, also he was the finest political leader ever.

The Supreme Court's decision to uphold the Affordable Care Act reflects a tragic misreading of the Constitution and the law, such which could cost us not just economic troubles, but also in terms of liberty. On the bright side, the Court recognized that there are limits to what Congress may do under the Commerce Clause. But this was the silver-lining of a dark cloud. The Court then fundamentally misreads the Affordable Care act, contorting facts to find another authority, the power to tax was designed for the Congress's ability to enact the law. The distress of the decision will be felt far beyond The Affordable Care Act, as the courts deception was beyond description and John Roberts multiple lies were outright incredible.

Thanks for the Heritage Foundation and for their marching to the same beat as mine, makes one feel like they and I are not the only ones in defense of our republic, when defense **should not** ever, become necessary.

I have faith in the arguments, principles and beliefs I have presented and now others must themselves become involved, acting to preserve the laws written in our Constitution, and the largest part of all, reinforcing and bringing God Almighty, back into our political system.

On a political note, I absolutely believe we need a new president, rather essentially we are in need of a man whos source and convictions come from God, with God given exceptional qualities. Strong men like Washington, Jefferson, Franklin, Adams, Monroe and Patrick Henry, on and on. We need not a new country, but an old country, the republic from which we originated. That one, great men fought for and two, our God given gift to We the People, a great republic, where is that republic today? Our country was Christian based and had only <u>one God</u>, it was pluralistic only in the sense of theological approach. Theology existence, occurs in four well-defined distinctions: one. _Divinity_ the science of God and divine things. Two, _morality_, divine laws and moral duties. Three being, _speculative_ teaching us the objects of faith. Four, _scholastics_ that which teaches by reasoning of the principles of faith. There were several approaches in different organizations, while all were Christians, believing in God and His Son Jesus Christ, His death and resurrection to pardon our sins.

Nowadays it's anything goes, as a society the moral condition possess no significant existence of quality, wayward and defiant at best in the secular realm. We need not turn our country around, what is required, is for us to explore those days when men were men, giving what was necessary regardless the cost, giving their whole to create a republic which was left for us to continue. Those men pledged their lives, fortunes and most of all their **sacred honor.** Where are any men of that measure at this very crucial time?

Thus begining to revolutionize this totally corrupt political system, one which We the People have created, therefore it's We the People who must return to God for guidance and from the ideals from where we began, to proceed in unison, fifty sovereign states together united as one under God Almighty, obligated to exercise power over the National Government, which we created. This I believe is the solitary path we are compelled to follow, in lieu of any other, in order to again be blessed by God Almighty. I'm certain at this moment you are exhausted from my poor ability to communicate quickly and more efficiently, for this I seriously apologize. Nevertheless, I have two brief (really) points to leave with you to consider.

First, the term Congressman, Congresswomen words coined a number of years ago and used constantly today. The word Congress in all six of my dictionaries state "a meeting place an assembly of delegates, a place where people of faith meet in congress, etc."

I'm not one to quibble... but these folks are Senators and Legislators elected in your home state, persons to meet in congress in Washington D.C., supposedly to represent you and me for our benefit, with and between the other 49 states. Joining mutually, to the best advantage of all the sovereign people and states. Remember, **we** are where it all is supposed to begin and deliberate, passing on our wishes to our Senators and Legislators, (House of Representatives).

Our seat of the national government, Washington D.C. a meeting place for our representatives, not their home. We are the only people in the world, with a meeting place not located in a certain city in a particular state. Our Founders appreciated and foreseen the challenge of the Constitutions and contrast between states, thus a neutral area being equal to all.

Secondly, dual citizenship, one being Washington D.C. since as I most folks live, reside, exercise our faith, work, play, etc. in one of the fifty sovereign states. I have a home in New Mexico and I decline to own property, or by any rational thought reside in Washington D.C. So the question I put forward, for what purpose or justification am I considered a citizen of Washington D.C., since it's to merely provide a meeting place (congress) for our representatives. Although in case law, occasionally they use this expression in their cases, as for myself, without merit.

Consider this for a moment, if all the Senators and Legislators, the Administration with all their bureaucrats and appointees, the Military, HHS, IRS, ACA HSS, DHS, FBI,CIA, NSI, Diplomats etc. you get the point, were to go home, now who I ask would we bequeath these ten square miles. Merely an asinine, trivial thought to lighten things up a bit, **perhaps?**

My point being, there are no Senators and House Legislators other than the citizens from your state, sent to Washington D.C. by the people of your state and a President plus his supporting cast, elected by you, rather not his cast. There is no other entity, only those we chose sending to Washington D.C., at that time considered the National Government, where Sovereign States United are supposed to work together for the benefit of each other's states. Then they return home to their families and their many occupations.

When this classified company of people return home, their obligation is reporting back to the citizens of the state of which they served. This is the precise reason there must be term limits, while after returning home they go back to their original occupation. People in service of their state should deem this position of service and ought to consider it a privilege, not an occupation.

I felt it necessary, in a well-defined matter to establish the correct words rather than those so often spoken, the incorrect idea of "well those people in Washington" as if there is some magical group of persons to lay blame upon. Well I'm here to tell all, there is only you and I to blame when factors seem out of our control, again suggesting it's just you and I here to fix or change those factors. We chose the people we send to meet in Washington to represent our interest and our wants if indeed our state is incapable. If that is unsuccessful and changing people does not succeed, there is yet another answer at Article five, read it, it's a Constitutional Convention held by the state Legislators or by a convention itself amending, thus creating a new Constitution. May I say, stop whining and complaining and do something.

This summing-up of reason, is specifically designated for those who may call themselves Christians, as they should be out front leading the way for the repair of our broken government. At this time ISIS above all needs our intense and relentless force, there is a need to change our combative posture, becoming extremely further aggressive in the middle-east, which includes Iran and Syria. It is irrational for us teaming up with Iran for any reason. When questioned during an interview about ISIS Dr. Jeffress pastor of the First Baptist Church in Dallas was asked, many Christian leaders believe in praying for peace as the answer for the middle-east. Dr. Jeffress replied, "I believe one must first pray, then kill them, as their ruthless brutal goal is to kill us and anyone who doesn't agree with their cold-blooded objectives, using some merciless religion as their perverse reasoning". I find myself, in total agreement with the pastor, as these vicious people comprehend one thing power and obliteration, how else could we approach this group of which I believe are depraved criminal people.

He also made clear that the Quran is a fake, noting over 35 verses that command Muslims to murder Jews and Christians who get in the way of Islam's jihad. The evidence in the Mid- East seems to support Dr. Jeffress position, as ISIS continues to slaughter Christians. This persists with little opposition in words or action from the President of the United States, he is incapable or unwilling to call out the perpetrators, still failing to call them for what they are, extreme Islamic terrorist and perhaps not only so called extreme Islam.

Now we are giving Iran 150 BILLION dollars as a reward for signing an agreement while we knelt before them giving away the farm, "so to speak", as of yet they have not signed. Why should we consider negotiations, we are in a strong position to demand, furthermore, Iran built their strength by lying and continue to create terrorism through the Middle-East, Northern Africa. Meanwhile Ayatollah Khamenei carries on calling for death to the Jews and the great Satan United States and we should grant them 150 Billion dollars, even Neville Chamberlain didn't give Hitler a signing bonus, Obama breaks new ground daily. This man Obama, is either the chief architect of buffoonery we ever had visited upon us, or a fool allocating innumerable funds to ever failing ideas, as if government was in business. Every public endeavor has been a boondoggle, his ability to implant, or guide in facilitating foreign affairs has been another disaster. The only other answer, he is intent on destroying this nation as a Christian republic. Let's remember as I have been critical of his early education, was Muslim, one can question easily his love for America while he persists to defend the Islam ideology regardless of the mealy-mouth lying words coming out from between his lips. .

Now he, Obama has entered into a compact with Iran over their nuclear build up. An episode not approved by congress nor supported by the American people, nevertheless he has moved ahead with the support of the U.N. and the European nations. The aftermath of this accord, without any doubt is horrendous to the free world, thus this agreement must be terminated.

Since details don't categorically dispense substance, the contract unquestionably does. It is at the heart of an argument over the character of U.S. leadership in the Middle East. Therefore it becomes significant and central due to the obvious implications and may come to be adrift in the struggle over centrifuges and enrichment percentages.

We find President Obama and this Iranian deal is the centerpiece of his adversely advised nuclear non-proliferation struggles, his effort to pull the United States from its earlier commitment in the destructive struggles of the region. He Obama, seeking to re-establish the United States as a balance in the arena of the middle east, rather than as an open participant in its endless civil wars. United States has no true friends, only true enemies it is able and willing to join. I see only that "the U.S. supports Iranian goals in Iraq, all the while supporting Iranian opponents in Yemen". It's so apparent moral transparency is loosely used by U.S. and its allies, entangling themselves in their disputes with Iran. This conundrum has befallen upon our nation through destitute, inferior leadership by President Obama, and a more often than not, a deficient congress.

As I write these words, Putin has moved fighter planes and anti-aircraft missiles into Syria to support the **Bashar Hafez al-Assad government**, as explained to our spineless President. One could go on and on, rather more exactly, unrequired to say as it would be senseless.

I must move on to the third part of my trilogy, trying to expose the many problems facing our republic. The sovereignty and safety of our republic and its citizen are at risk, whither they grasp it or not, moreover the lack of God Almighty in our society allows socialism to enter the vacuum left by the absence of God and His leadership plus His very presence. This nation as with all nations, God Almighty must reside in that nation, both its people and government in order to maintain a sense of moral integrity. I believe the problem within our society stems from self-indolence in so many ways. Weak Christians revealed by all the near empty churches, and a good number of pastors displaying an anemic account of Jesus Christ and His redeeming love. Furthermore, our present government's attack on Christianity comes from all directions as well, in which again stems from socialism.

The President advises us to acknowledge the Muslim religion while he would not acknowledge the beheading of Christians in Iraq by ISIS.

This republic was founded on the blood of men who believe in Jesus Christ and God Almighty including the general who led the battle against England. George Washington stated "The Continental Congress having ordered Friday, the 17th instant, to be observed as a day of "Fasting, Humiliation, and Prayer, humbly to supplicate the mercy of Almighty God, that it would please him to pardon all our manifold sins and transgressions and finally establish the peace and freedom of America upon a solid and lasting foundation."

## Part Three

### Restitutions for our Republic succumbing to Socialism, then begin to restore God's values to our Republic, a Republic God's wisdom hath created

Upon an honest and factual example as a portion of the national government's utter corruption, one should respond. My accusations regarding the Affordable Care Act, exposing Chief Justice John Roberts as an example of corruption at the highest levels. Therefore, while exposing where government has been unmasked, both correctly and objectively, thus as a result giving you the reader, a clear explanation of how this particular act came to fruition. Consequently through corruption and proven to be propagated by lies and deception from the mouth of Chief Justice John Roberts. Therefore, Justice Roberts has not only exposed himself, while in addition a few others honest enough to render the facts as written, not necessarily by brilliance, rather honesty and challenging work. Mine established through a *Fiat Justitia* case, against Chief Justice John Roberts of the U.S. Supreme Court, writing the assenting decision on cases, docs. *11-398, 11-393, 1-400* all involving a part of the Patient Protection and Affordable Care Act and other things. In particular with the utmost significance, "the individual mandate". Anyone reading my presentation today and studying our history, therefore subsists as indisputable evidence, as one of many remarkable finds, just how numerous cases the Supreme Court have convoluted through manipulation and in other instances through outright lies. These individuals in black robes have held sovereignty for themselves. Therefore being of a contrary mind, while feigning allegiance to our Constitution and many through their actions have diminished our Constitution and thus in particular failed the American people, again.

I carefully and exactingly spent an abundance of time endeavoring to share my aspirations for an America of past ideals, given to us by God, therefore expecting

102

those beliefs would direct our nation toward honest and careful selection into a healthier and again Christian Republic. This selection which will rekindle that salient desire, a hunger for our lost republic, not terminated rather merely lost, which will again bring the yearnings for freedom and liberty back to all, as it's still alive. As a demonstration that we have unalienable rights, granted by God our ultimate leader, not government nor society, our entire destiny, as a matter of fact is in His will, plus being the impetus to seize and secure personal freedom, thus savoring them once more, these are ours to regain.

Since our Constitution has fallen onto the hands of those who wish to trash it, to the point it seems invalid, regardless of what politicians from both sides and especially the President's attempt to sell you the idea that we are a democracy, nevertheless our Constitution exist and we are a Republic, granted to us by the God of His universe. What's more God bestowed upon us unalienable rights, <u>AMONG</u> them Life, Liberty and the pursuit of happiness. These words are solidified guarantees granting us total freedom, freedom from government as they are meant to be our servant, since it's by the people for the people, of the people. We have been designed by God to be the masters of our future according to His guide lines, government being our servant, is meant to follow the wishes and desires of "We the People".
Rather today as I have stated before one must connect this truth to ourselves, government is a poor and unfaithful servant, unfortunately a true persona of the people's national government. As a result the situation appears the same, government's intent is to extinguish our Constitution and enslave the people with decrees, regulations and ultimately more importantly, trash the word of God attempting to destroy Christianity in our republic.

The protests, rioting, and insane police response in Ferguson has only escalated overnight, but Fox & Friends invited **Jonathan Gentry**, a minister whose "viral video" <u>rant</u> (a poor word used to express their implied message) criticized the black community for not obeying the police. His words are straight to the point, something that President Barack Obama should have finished, so many days prior. **Gentry** wrote lately on his <u>Facebook</u> page: A Man said to him *"You're dragging us blacks down!" I said sir, You can't possibly go any lower than where you already are. You come to my Facebook page, I'm Stepping Your Game Up!! The reason you hate me is because I don't cater to your ignorance and degenerate mindset. Enough is Enough!!!…It's your own actions & behavior that's keeping you bound, stuck, not getting ahead. Everything you stood for went down the drain last night by burning down your own community.*

*"Your iniquities have turned these blessings away, and your sins have kept good from you." (Jeremiah 5:25) "I'm going to tell you what you need to hear as opposed to what you want to hear," "All we know how to do is blame the police and white folks for our actions. All we know how to do is protest march and riot and loot. I'm sick of it! I'm sick of it!"*

Simply put these words are true for all Americans, the method of our actions may be expressed by different means, but before God there is no difference and they persist in bringing the same feeble and pathetic arguments. I mean both blacks and whites persons.

Please, if nothing else remember Jesus Christ is our redeemer, individually and as a nation, there is none other. When one wishes to protest, bring your protest before God first. It would appear there are many who would seek to twist the truth, leading us down a slippery path, while obliterating our republic into chaos and many bandits waiting to suck the life out of those persons looking for the passage to freedom. The answers are all written in the Bible and our Constitution. What needs to happen, remains for us to follow them and demand our appointed officials to follow **our** lead, as it is the people who are the true leaders.

Moving ahead, President Obama being the true architect of deliberate false statements, without question a perpetrator of lies and a man devoid of morals. Furthermore, in his earlier years was thoroughly engrossed as a student and disciple of Saul Alinsky ( a gangster and a member of the old Al Capone mob), Hillary Clinton as well, perhaps even more so writing her college thesis and dissertation on his life and ideas, whom she esteemed while prizing him for his revolutionary assertions. An example of words from one Saul Alinsky *"The rules make the difference between being a realist radical and being a rhetorical one, advancing ones radical goals by camouflaging them, change your style to appear to be working within the system".* Simply looking around one will easily see this theory in play today, mainly by the President, as he has often spoken words knowing they were lies, in many cases attempting to manipulate their meaning. The terrorist ISIS employ the same ideology as Saul Alinsky. Place this on your calendar, I believe him, Obama to be a plausible blooming prospect of become the precursor to the anti-Christ.

We need to take hold of the national government's abuse of the Constitution, knowing those who cherry-pick it, then choose to exploit the laws. Furthermore, we must not allow government to manipulate our faiths, ideas and activities, therefore taking our soveriegnty by subjugation, thus stealing our true source of strength through faith in God, the same God which gave wisdom and power to the founders of this once great republic, yearning again for His will to become our strength.

Consequently, I have chosen to apply the same implication of prosecution by *Fiat Justitia,* as previously were applied in opposition to Justice John Roberts's deceptive opinions.

Even though there exist a profuse supply of infractions by our President, acting outside the law and over reaching his authority, plus there is an abundant amount of exploitations for him to defend presently. However, an example of the crimes, violations and infractions of laws he has commited still exist.

These proceedings are from a substantial list of absolute lawlessness, a *modus injuria*. The only imperatives are the overabundance of illegal issues he indulged himself, the selection of egregious measures we have chosen, yet are from so abundant a list that it becomes problematic. We have decide upon those from not only laws he has broken, but laws which he failed to apply and enforce. This servant's many obligations and debt to the Constitution and the people of our republic.

Therefore, believing the significance of injury to our citizens becomes first and foremost, the uttermost of substantive questions, though this may depend on a person's individual prospective, as to what, where or who and the adverse damage Obama has willfully inflicted which has hustled up many criminal activities. The ones I have chosen are but a few of those which could be exposed. I hope these will paint a picture of the immoral heart of this man, one Barack Obama, whom is not a Negro, rather a Mulatto, merely a man playing to the Negro gallery, pursuing their votes and espousing their needs as a Black, but doing nothing, he simply is a *perfidus une,* Latin for betrayal of trust.

Thus in my judgment I believe President Obama is a psychopathically motivated person, and so characterized by his delusional fantasies, these generally stem from some belief system, where he judges by fiat, thus blaming America for the wrongs in the world, for reason of its power and influence in world affairs. His feeling of omnipotence, further showing his obsession with himself and his grandiose ideas therefore being a licentious person, a true megalomaniac.


I have read the above statement several times to revisit the words, considering all the issues involved. As for myself, each fits Obama's character and personality, and are an absolute projection of this very flawed person. Nevertheless, I am myself a sinful .person finding myself carrying out sinful gambits and deeds, then again I am a Christian and God through His mercy will forgive, rather I pray for His forgiveness and attempt with His help to improve, therefore being remorseful.

I see no repentance in any of his actions, on the contrary Obama as President is obligated, as a result of his own actions, choses to be meritoriously held to the highest of standards, these rules and conceptions exist without omission, yet Obama has broken all.

I will commence with my charges against President Obama in *Fait Justitia,* exposing his lawless behavior hence, the precondition, for certain a prerequisite for his being removed from office. Therefore, after my charges and expectation of an successful impeachment, the Supreme Court must bring charges of treason, as the man is a traitor to our republic.

# First accusation

This concerns his failure to maintain his oath of office.

When one reads our Constitution at Article two, section one, last clause it reads, ***"I do solemnly swear that I will faithfully execute the office of President of the United States and will to the best of my ability, preserve, protect and defend the Constitution of the United States."*** In all areas he has broken our trust and his promis, seems unwilling to have little or no concern for the people for which he has chosen to work. This is by law *juris gentium* "Of the law of nations". An oath or affirmation for truth of statement, which, when one renders himself willfully asserting untrue statements, must be punished for perjury, as it seems this individual guilty on the face of the facts, these accusation stand. ....Penial code at 241.1...Gatewood v State 15 Md. App.341, 291A.2d, 551,553...*Vaughn v. State, 146 Tex. Cr.R 586,177 S.w.2d 59,60 and others*

Furthermore, while reading these many statutes it behooves us to keep the meaning relevant, *"Ratio est legis anima; mutatalegis ratione mutatur et lex. " ("The reason for the law is its soul; when the reason for the law changes, the law changes as well).* So if the soul of the law remains unchanged, the law endures. I have chosen to write those words first in Latin, not to muddy the waters, rather for stressing their importance and for future use of particular laws as Latin being a dead language, thus its meaning endures.

*We* citizens ought to pressure our people in Congress to consider the point of removing him from office. At least an attempt would show the world, especially our allies where this republic stands and its policies coexist with them.

## Second Accusation

<u>President Obama has failed to identify with the Constitution, acting as if a king</u>
Moreover the Constitution reads at Article One, first section, *"All legislative Powers herein granted shall be vested in a Congress of the United States, which will consist of a Senate and House of Representatives."* Plus Article One sec.8, where we find these powers are enumerated, moreover the President is NEVER mentioned.

Again we find at Article One section eight, the *"Congress will make All Laws which shall be necessary and proper for carrying into execution the foregoing Powers, and all other Powers vested by this Constitution in the government of the United States, or in any department or Officer thereof."*

In all of the described Articles above, President Obama has willfully rejected, with a defiant disregard for the laws created by the Congress, while exhibiting absolute contempt for the Constitution, these actions are considered, *contempt of Congress and shall be guilty of a misdemeanor and subject to a maximum $1,000 fine and 12 month imprisonment. At 2 U.S.C.A. sec. 192 also sec.194 in accordance with U.S. Am 9-90 020 Definition*

Congress has the authority to hold a person in contempt if the person's conduct or action obstructs the proceedings of Congress or, more usually, an inquiry by a committee of Congress.

*Case law: Quinn v. U.S., 349 U.S. 155, 75 S. Ct. 668, 99 L. Ed. 964, 51 A.L.R.2d 1157 (1955).*

Furthermore, at the moment he finds it primarily essential to avoid the serious situation at our southern border, where children are abandoned and criminals crossing by the hundreds. Meanwhile the House passes an unfortunate bill to help alleviate the problem, the only purpose was pandering to our citizens, without any chance of passing, therefore without purpose on the very face of its intended purpose. The Senate and House leaves for vacation and the President makes ready to follow.

In spite of the fact that the Mid-East is on fire and our borders open to all and our economy still in shambles, these remnants, these ashes are given to burnout, exposing the true interest of our national government. These depraved departure proceedings are appalling, as our nation is floundering due to self-indulgent and flawed leadership. While all persons need a period of rest, but is not an appropriate or inconspicuous objective while these serious and distressful needs go unattended. Absence to these necessary questions are not the answer, but the most disgraceful moment to depart Washington D.C. I feel it quite astonishing while egotistical or indifferent at best, thus for those reasons and a Congress which closes their eyes to such a situation, are in my opinion there goes the government We the People have chosen to work on our behalf.

## Third Accusation

<u>President Obama's willingness to defy Congress</u>
Let's remember Nancy Pelosi words, **We have to pass the (health care) bill so you can find out what is in it"**. So nobody read it and it passed and to this day not one of our leaders knows what's in it, including Nancy Pelosi. We are able to see what's in the title**, Patient Protection** and Health Care <u>Act and Other Things</u>. Clearly it is not about health care, rather insurance plans and what are the "Other Things"? Think about those words and refocusing upon words in this title.

Refocusing on the charges submitted against President Obama, as with his willfulness changing *HR 3962 being a part of, p.l. 111-148 at section 4980H (a) IRS CODE 1986* Affordable Care Act. This law became effective on Jan. 1 2014. He, Obama redefied the law and willfully and illegally granted to all corporations, with fifty or more full time employees an extension of the law for a period of one year. This violation is criminal on its face, an impeachable offence, described at Article Two, section Two, fourth clause, U.S. Constitution. This wanton and illegal act to which solitary action is fundamentally to be accomplished by the Congress alone, at ***Article 1 sec. 1 of the U.S. Constitution.*** *Juris effectus, " the effectiveness of a law is in its execution".* Any change in tax rates, no matter how small, must be proposed in Congress, passed by both chambers, then signed by the President into law. Which was the consequence. By the way, the same is true of government spending. The President cannot spend more than was authorized by Congress. The President can however, cut spending in any of his departments, unless Congress stated that he cannot. The merits of this accusation proves the President has little concern for the law, consequently it's the responsibility of Congress to act upon this violation *Article Two, section four* spells out the responcabilty of Congress; nevertheless again the court used their tricky unconstitutionality, found no place, anywhere, a figment of their imagination.

# Fourth Accusation

**Subsides to help persons unable to pay for Affordable care Act**
**HEALTH PLAN, A PART OF SECTION 1401 (Generally called subsides)**
At (2), (A)

(1) IN GENERAL. The term 'premium *assistance* credit amount' means, with respect to any taxable year, the sum of the premium assistance amounts determined under paragraph with respect to all coverage months of the taxpayer occurring during the taxable year.

(2) PREMIUM ASSISTANCE AMOUNT A premium assistance amount determined under this subsection with respect to any coverage month is the amount equal to the lesser of—
(A) the monthly premiums for such month for 1 or more qualified health plans offered in the **individual market within a State** which cover the taxpayer, the taxpayer's spouse, or any dependent (as defined in section 152) of the taxpayer and which were enrolled in through an
**Exchange established by the State** under 1311 of the Patient Protection and Affordable Care Act, or
(B) the excess (if any) of—
(1)     The adjusted monthly premium for such month for the applicable second lowest cost silver plan with respect to the taxpayer, over
(2)     An amount equal to 1/12 of the product of the applicable percentage and the

Tax payers household income for the taxable year.


This law in itself is self-explanatory and is written specifically for State exchanges, persons which were enrolled through an individual market, within a State exchange as defined in the Affordable Care Act. The law was written and emphatically intended, to address the problem which developed when less than a quarter of the States established an exchange, therefore the remaining 36 states would subsist without subsides. This created an enormously complex financial boondoggle for the national government..

Now President Obama believes otherwise, twisting his own intent, as he assumed all

States would establish their own exchanges, **presto,** we watch while he is determined to continue, unlawfully and willfully misapplying subsides in order to cover all exchanges, both state and federal.

This misuse of his own making, which his own blundering and again misjudging, caused havoc and hardships in taxes for We the People.

In my opinion this issue need not be heard by the Supreme Court, this law is so well defined there is no disputed case or scope for standing, purely clear and simple facts on their face value.

*Once more deliberately and defiantly with wanton disregard of the law as written. An impeachable offence as he has acted in deliberate disobedience of the law. Article Two sec. 4 U.S. Constitution again stipulates the action to be taken. "Removed from office by impeachment" and 1, 25 "possibly conviction of treason, bribery and other crimes and misdemeanors after impeachment."* This charge has value on the face of its proceedings and substance and it should be acted upon as it was originally meant and intended.

Nevertheless, the Supreme Court again decided to use "Judicial Deference" willfully, with disregard for the written law, change that which was originally paramount in the fundamental idea concerning this issue.

# Fifth Accusation

*U.S.. SUPREME COURT at 259 U.S. 20* **Bailey**
**vs. Drexel Furniture Co.**
**Decided May15, 1922... Syllabus**
*An act of Congress which clearly on its face, is designed to penalize, and hereby to discourage or suppress, conduct the regulation of which is reserved by the Constitution exclusively to the states, cannot be sustained under the federal taxing power by calling the penalty a tax, as appropriately explained previously. P.259 U.S. 37, 533: McCRAY vs. UNITED STATES, 195 U.S.27; Flint vs. Stone Tracy Co., 220 U.S. 107*

President Obama in violation of a legal instrument transposing a tax to punish, clearly designed for coercion by convoluting the word penalty into tax. Thereby accepting and exploiting a legal regulation reserved exclusively to the states by the Constitution. This idea cannot prevail on the facts. Simply by using federal taxing power by calling a penalty a tax are not facts. Regardless he has chosen to continue this unlawful activity, defiantly ignoring the Constitution.

The conflict involved is not problematic, it is again merely a misuse of the law as written in Article Two, section one, last clause...*faithful execute the Office of the President of the United States, and will to the best of my ability, preserve, protect and defend the Constitution of the United States".* While failing to perform his duties as written, he, President Obama is in direct violation of his obligation there imposed. Here again we find President Obama is derelict in his duties and to his oath of Office.

*Impeachment turns on the meaning of the phrase in the Constitution at Art. II Sec. 4, "Treason, Bribery, or other high Crimes and Misdemeanors".*
*I have carefully researched the origin of the phrase "high crimes and misdemeanors" and it's meaning to the Framers. I found the essential key for the understanding its*

*true meaning is the word "high". It does not mean "more serious". It refers to those punishable offenses which only apply to high persons, that is, to public officials, those who because of their official status, are under special obligations ".* Professor Roland

*We find in Article Two, section four,* provisions for the punishment for the failure to comply with the fore mentioned *"Article Two, sec.one clause nine".* President Obama has perverted the Constitution by forcing a person or group of persons, conforming to a command, where choice ought to remain the essence and yet this concept is not to be found within the U.S. Constitution. Webster's dictionary defines *"comply to yield, to fulfill, to be obsequious".* Furthemore: **Intent to mislead.** The witness must know that the testimony is false and must give it with the intent to mislead the court. **Only false statements are perjury.** False testimony that results from testimony may be perjury if one of the conflicting statements is necessarily false (and prosecutors can prove perjury without proving *which one* is false). A person convicted of perjury under federal law may face up to five years in prison and fines. **Extrinsic fraud:** *Deception that is collateral to the issue being considered; intentional misrepresentation outside the transaction itself, depriving one party or (groups of persons)of informed consent or full participation. C.S.J. sec. 309 at 375, 441,(1)* Famous persons committing perjury have their cases dismissed and seldom pay for their crimes, furthermore, 14th amendment section 1, here we find the President willfully violating and in breach of the U.S. Constitution. Moreover I believe President Obama has no attachment to our republic, has broken his oath, therefore willfully contravened our laws, due to his thinking, laws are but a repugnancy. This only suggest that his intent to disregard the law thus on its face is repugnant. **Swan vs, The United States:** *contradiction in allegation of material facts. 3 wyo.151,9 p931 and 27Am ju stat 110,41 p.l. at 47.*

## Sixth Accusation

President Obama's procedures fly in the face of 14th Amendment, section 3 last half, again his total and absolute defiance of any laws, he may find obstructive to his ideology, devour and destroy any ability for reasonable considerations. His exchange of a deserter (whose intent and action was to join the enemy) for five enemy combatants released from Guantonamo without the consent or foregoing the required consultation of Congress. This without anxiety for all his reckless immoral acts and lack of pretense of intent, went with reference to socialism. The violation of the 14th amendment is an added deliberate law broken without hesitation or remorse. The congress must gather the courage and become a part of the appropriate engagement in *Article Two sec. four, of these matters and brought by means of the Constitution's intention, where it enhances the essential need for Impeachment proceedings.*

## Seventh Accusation

The fraud perpetrated upon the American people by President Obama, were he lies and expounds so habitually, stating *"If you like your Doctor you can keep your Doctor, if you like your health plan, you can keep your health plan"* etc., *this knowing full well he was lying, is called perjury, an instance of deliberately lying, making material false and /or misleading.*

*Cases... Criminal Justice System - perjury 1 sections 2-23, 5-8-21*

Deception/fraud: fraud being an intentional perversion of truth, for the purpose of inducing another person in reliance upon it, to part with a valuable thing belonging to him, or to surrender legal rights.

*Johnson v McDonald 170 Okl.117,39 P2d, 150... Citizen Standard Life insurance. Gilly Tex.Civ. Civ.App521 S.W.2d 354,356.*

115

*Deception; the act of intentional misleading by falsehoods spoken, are synonymous with fraud.* Jackman vs. Mau at *78 C. A. 234, 177 P. 2d 599, 605. Knowingly and willfully making a false statement pertaining to a present or past existing fact. …Intenio inservire non leges intentioni.* The intention of the person ought to be subservient to the law, not the law to the intention.

Noah Webster; perversion, *"one who is obstinate in the wrong, disposed to be contrary, distorted from the correct". Action ex delicto; an action arising from a breach of duty, coming from out of a contract. McCullough vs. the American workman: 200 S.C., 84, 20 S.E. 2d 640*

The accumulative action of deception, fraud and perversion are in fact treason, or of betraying the state into the hands of a foreign power. Treason consisting of two elements. Adherence to the enemy and rendering him aid, abetting him and granting him comfort…*Cramer v U.S. , US, N.Y.325 U.S,1, 65Ct. 918,932,89 L eD,1441 see U.S.C.A. at 2381* President Obama commited these crimes and then some. According to the Constitution, *punishment shall be set by Congress and shall have Power to declare the Punishment of Treason, but no Attainder of Treason shall work Corruption of Blood, or Forfeiture except during the Life of the Person attainted….* Where or what aligns or is in conjunction with these activities, lays our President. Shall it be fraud, deception or perversion? The protection of the two-witness rule of the Constitution in such case extends at least to all acts of the defendant which are used to draw incriminating inferences that aid and comfort have been given. P. 325 U. S. 33. In a prosecution upon an indictment charging treason by adhering to enemies of the United States, giving them aid and comfort, in violation of § 1 of the Criminal Code two of the overt acts alleged and relied on were: P. 325 U. S. 34.

Since the president resides in this Republic, therefore is subject the same laws as all citizens, I am of discovery while this accusation has merit under this code, however his tenure will expire prior to an indictment.

116

## Eighth Accusation

<u>Possibility of aiding and comforting the enemy</u>

With respect to the Bergdahl exchange for five Taliban leaders, flaunting Bergdahl in front of the nation as a prize. Had the President followed this simple requirement, one that **he** signed into law, following this need for responsibility, then many of the dangers posed by this decision could have been avoided altogether.

Hence as part of the, *2014 National Defense Authorization Act and the Consolidated Appropriations Act of 2014,* he defied this Act, willfully and remains in violation thereof. He is required to consult with congress by law regarding such matters. This again is an unlawful deed and along with his numerous and various disregard for our Constitution, demonstrates his lack of love for our republic and it's exceptional "republican form of governing" , plus its continuing ideals.

However he, in his willful defiant attitude not having any respect for this law, again on the face of his refusal to conform is in non- compliance with *Maestas v. American Metal Co. of New Mexico 37 n.m. 203 20P.2d 924, 94*

*"Do not separate text from historical background. If you do, you will have perverted and subverted the Constitution, which can only end in a distorted, bastardized form".*
*James Madison*

## Ninth Accusation

### The question of treason, by political action of a President.

Now the five terrorist Obama released from Gitmo will in all probability return to the battle field and we the people were again deceived, what's more the deserter Bergdahl has been charged with desertion, found guilty but not sentenced.

*It is not often that a soldier who deserted his post in the face of the enemy has five Taliban Guantánamo detainees exchanged for his release from captivity, is welcomed back to the United States, and has the president's national security adviser praise him for having served his country "with honor and distinction."* New York Times

My question supposed, for the action by the President is indeed of treasonous proceedings (through highly political biased manner) therefore, a deliberate and premeditated behavior. Thus for this reason be charged accordingly, by the Congress. Treason: *an act of attempting to over through the government of a state to which one owes allegiance. [ cases: treason C. J. S. 1, 2-3, 5]...* U.S. Code › Title 18 › Part I › Chapter 115 › § 2381

# Tenth Accusation

<u>Penetration of our southern borders, failure to deal with this breach.</u>

Our southern borders remain unprotected, yet President Obama has chosen to use a spurious, unconstitutional act to create a hoax played on millions of illegal immigrants. America shares 7,000 miles of land border with Canada and Mexico, as well as rivers, lakes and coastal waters around the country. These borders are vital economic gateways that account for trillions of dollars in trade and travel each year. They are also home to some of our nation's largest and safest cities and communities. Protecting our borders from the illegal movement of weapons, drugs, contraband, and people, while promoting lawful entry and exit, is essential to homeland security, economic prosperity, and national sovereignty. Border incursions by violent drug smugglers and other criminals are the primary issue here. To protect against these criminals, the U.S. government is by Constitutional law required to secure borders (for all the above reasons). Patrols in the Southwest have substantially increased the amount of drugs, guns, and cash seized over the last three years. We the People have allowed our national government, in particular the lack of real Presidential action and the absence of concern it's self with this issue of illegal immigrants and procuring for them entitlements meant for citizens of our nation only, as <u>we the people</u> have clearly earned the right to enjoy them.

The Constitution clearly defines the responsibility of government to protect its citizens from dangers within and witho*ut: "Article four sec.4 The United States shall guarantee to every State in this Union a Republican Form of Government, and shall protect each of them against Invasion; and on Application of the Legislature, or of the Executive (*when the Legislature cannot be convened*)*
Obviously President Obama has failed again to honor another segment of the Constitution.

This obligation and the function of the House and Senate remains; *"an impeachable offense for the Commander in Chief to disobey this clear and unequivocal command of the U.S. Constitution." See Chapter 8 U.S.C.A. 1101 (a) (15). The term 'immigrant' means every alien... except an alien who is an ambassador, public minister, or career diplomatic.* May also be an alien other than one coming for the purpose of study or of performing skilled or unskilled labor or as a representative of foreign press, radio, film, or other foreign information, for that matter all the media.

The above persons are in our country by passport, visa etc. and have no intent of permanently settling here in this place or point. "Furthermore, an illegal immigrant is a criminal, as *in chapter 8 U.S.C.A. at SECTION 1325, ONE, enters at the wrong time or place, TWO, eludes examination by immigration officers, or THREE, obtains entry by fraud"*. Thus becoming illegitimate persons in our nation due to their actions and the failure of the President to follow Article 4 sec. 4 as stated earlier in an above paragraph illegal *per se*, unlawful in and of itself, and not because of some extraneous circumstance. *Schmitt v. Wright, 317 Ill. App. 384, 48N.E.2d 184, 192 and Natural soda co. v. city of Los Angeles Cal App, 132, P. 2d 553,563* or perhaps better yet I say, simply impeach him, as this will prevent further destruction of our republic and our Constitution.

# Eleventh Accusation

Benghazi events exist today as before since both President Obama and Sect. Hillary Clinton have failed to correct their lies…De placate; *of a plea, or in an action.* Formal words used in the declarations and other proceedings, as descriptive of the particular action brought. *Deliberately, willfully with premeditation, intentionally and purposely decieved. Averheart vs state, 158 Ark. 639, 238 S.W. 620, 021 Therefore, by the exhibit of the facts, thus arrange the given merit to entertain this case.*

So acted the President along with Sect, Hillary Clinton knowingly with intention of continuing their lies about Benghazi, over the four caskets of fallen American heroes at Andrews Air Force base. The President stated an anti-Muslim tape made by an American, generated the attack in Benghazi, knowing he was with mendacity contending that the taped video gave impetus for the attack, which knowingly was deliberately and falsely indicated, as they knew it was an act of terrorism.

As Chief Executive of our republic, he is the representative of our people and is morally obligated to act thusly. He knowingly, willfully and intentionally lied to the love ones of these fallen heroes, defying the law and morality. As stated before, all laws broken, (parted by violence through word or action) by anyone including the President, is at least a misdemeanor, thus should be treated as such an impeachable offence. *Gatewood vs. state, 15 MD 314, 290A.2d 551,553 Since perjury is a crime when a lawful oath is administered to a person who swears willfully and absolutely falsely, in a matter material to an issue, point in question If he believes it not to be true.... Subornation of perjury is procuring another to commit perjury. 18 USCA at 1622.* These are both crimes and should be punished appropriately, for a president it would be impeachment. As she Hillary, has also become obligated for punishment and ought to have been removed from office. Two years after her tenure in office we find Hillary still has her own email and secret server, instead of the official government, Email. Why?

## Twelfth Accusation

The lack of human decency or concern by President Obama, this for the multitude of Christians whom were slain, raped, and incapacitated, the savagery placed on display for the world to view. The president's argument is that distinguishing between Muslim and Christian refugees would be "shameful." As a question of national security, that is a difficult argument to sustain: While in the United States and Western Europe, Christian refugees have not become terrorists and it's a simple fact that their admission does not present "a clear and present danger", the same security risk does not exist. That does not mean all Muslim refugees should not be admitted, but it does suggest that an adamant refusal to distinguish among refugees on religious lines is illogical. Furthermore, vetting the Muslim from Syria is impossible. Indeed the President in his remarks in Turkey is proud of that blindness, and calls any special efforts to rescue Christians "shameful," at least until we have reliable vetting procedures for Muslims.

I am a firm believer, that President Obama is himself a Muslim. He was raised and taught in Muslim schools in Jakarta, where he lived with his stepfather. **Jakarta, Indonesia** (CNN) -- Indonesians have paid tribute to Barack Obama on the eve of his acceptance of the Nobel Peace Prize. A statue of the U.S. President, who lived in Jakarta, has been unveiled in a park in the Indonesian capital. Obama received this peace prize after six months in office.

I suppose my question remains consistently unchanged, why have evangelical Christians been so quiet for so long? Rather than praying hard then becoming seriously involved, pressing Congress, funding the action for Christian refugees being brought into our fold. I am unapologetic for consistently selecting true Christians to criticize regarding these matters, we are the people who are required to respond, these challenges, as Christ Jesus commanded. Then again God told Moses "quit praying I have heard your words, get the people moving, march forward". Exodus:14, 15-18 Then from the Life Application Bible explanation, "Lord told Moses to stop praying and get moving".

## Part Three Plus

People in Germany have been warned to stay away from their windows and to refrain from waving during Barack Obama's visit later this month. Local residents will face a number of limitations on the weekend of 23 and 24 will be set up as a security zone.

Those who wish to pass through the two access roads may have to undergo vehicle checks and carry a passport with them. During his visit, Mr Obama will also discuss the Transatlantic Trade and Investment Partnership. But before landing in Germany, the President will visit Saudi Arabia and the UK. This while the middle-east burns.

I must say I was not at all surprised when President Obama was in Cuba playing footsie with Fidel Castro and watching a baseball game. Whereas Brussels was mourning a terrorist attack the president decided to continue watching baseball in communist Cuba. Then flying to Buenos Aires he and wife Michele partied while dancing across the floor doing the tango. To say that he is disengaged from reality is pure complexities of irony, this in his tenure in office. Obama has advanced these actions into a skill over the past seven and one half years, as he winds down his last year in office, while failing the people of our Republic and the office of the presidency.

I find his proceedings conflicts with American values and at least make note of the procedures of any progress, as he represents our nation to the entire world. However, this in all probability remains of little consequence to him, as his real mindset is his personal legacy, rather than the one he's wanting is but signs of failure.

President Obama's unparalleled desire to close Gitmo penal complex is another of his acts of criminal behavior and believed to be an act directly intended for criminal proceedings to apply, as the facts appear we are still at war with a group of Islamic nations which continues to this day. The international Wars Act states, as the American government claims that the facility was not covered by the Geneva Conventions, protecting prisoners of war as the detainees were "enemy combatants".

It is now clear that the CIA allowed water-boarding, now has again been considered by congress and has not been used for over 10 years.

*The treaties of 1949 were ratified, in whole or with **reservations**, **by 196 countries**. Moreover, the Geneva Convention also defines the rights and protections afforded to **non-combatants**, yet, because the Geneva Conventions are about people in war, while the U.S. POSITION IS ENEMEY COMBATANTS FAIL TO DIFFER FROM UNIFORMED PERSONS, as most combatants are not uniformed, the articles of the Geneva convention do not address __warfare__ proper, further stated the idea of POWs be able to be held till the end of hostilities. My source the "Geneva Convention" It appears this situation is unclear and they never addressed a situation so twisted, fragmented and disjointed prior to these conditions.* When we are talking about a "war on terror", they now have black uniforms, a black flag and Califate a simple form of governing. *U.S. Code › Title 18 › Part I › Chapter 115 › § 2381*

Regardless of our loathing and repugnance for them. I am of the opinion they have an army and any captured and held till we kill all the others, then given what need be bestowed upon them, a trial, executed and buried in a mass unmarked grave.

President Obama has produced for himself a convoluted extension into another **phase**, a moment in time to show himself a fool, while attempting to destroy our republic.


The obvious action for this particular issue as in prior events, impeachment. Deceit; *Walter vs. state 2080 Ind, 231, 195 NE"* Furthermore, the act of *intentional deception, misleading by falsehood spoken or acted Jackson vs Mau 78 C.A., 177, 234 P2d599 605.* Destroy: *State v Robinson, 266 Minn. 166, 123, N.W.* 2d 812.

When reviewing this issue, for me the outlook is perplexing and without much doubt a challenging situation, significantly since ISIS has determind themselves a nation.

With this twelfth charge I will finish, otherwise one could go on and on without any further demonstrative affect or influence, exclusive of necessity or motive. In my *Fiat Justitia* charges against Justice John Roberts, this was a single case for which I researched extensively, presented many facts, whereas the twelve charges against

President Obama I only scratched the surface, since it would require an entire book to submit all the facts regarding his lies, deceit, dereliction of duty, creating his own law and violating those in which he disapproved. Regarding bills passed in the House and sent to the Senate, his lackey Harry Reid refused to bring forward some 350 bills to the Senate for consideration, no veto necessary. As stated there seems no end to his mendacious misrepresention and fabrications of activity, accordingly I will proceed no farther with this particular endeavor with charges of Obama life's goal, that of *"fundamentally transforming the United States of America",* as so he stated.

My attention remains upon Barack Obama's exploits as a result of *his* impression of authority, therefore I question his recent action trading prisoners with Cuba, this without the knowledge or the consent of Congress. Asserted he would setup an embassy in Cuba and begin trade negotiations, these proceedings all happening by executive action a week before Christmas, this while Congress was not in session. After more than fifty years without political relationship, this sudden change is merely a move on Obama's part to further his scheme or the perception of "relevance" in the affairs of our republic.

Now we are beginning a new Senate and House the 6th of January 2015 which will be controlled by the GOP, Obama will continue to attempt making laws and breaking ones in existence, with his agenda in disarray and amid little help from his own party he will resist and fight like a cornered wild beast, of which he persists in subsisting. This was his training as a community organizer, his background as a youth in Kenya and the study of Saul Alinsky's theories. How different could his response have been but to revolt, after the past seven years and the minimal resistance from the conservative members of Congress? I believe we are in for a critical and dangerous year ahead, I hope this new congress is up to this situation. Moreover we are facing a transformation of a relation with those wanting radical change without dialogue, this of course creates the need for more police to maintain some avenue for peace and order and protecting all citizens including the out of control protesters. These problems and many others steming from the forefront of the illegal behavior of Obama and his staff thus giving false reason for radical protesters to exploit the First

Amendment. The First Amendment states no such idea of protest as we see today, as simply and justly reads, *"the right of the people to peaceably assemble and to petition the government for a redress of grievances"* and of course freedom of *speech,* however, this suggestion of being speech has by no means any class of a narrative, it will only lead to anarchy, that seems to me is where our society is heading.

It is my opinion Congress needs the fortitude to place loyalty, veracity and legitimacy to our nation far ahead of party loyalty, as a result impeaching Obama consequently stripping off a layer of impurities from the quasi Constitution and reverting to the orginal, plus removing him from office, now. Obama's most recent remarks regarding the NYC grand jury decision, denies respect to their police, an incident which was totally race driven. This merely powered people to protest deeper into adverse situations, copiously guided by Al Sharpton a mere punk at best and the devil in all likelihood. As we listen to the chanting of KILL THE COPS, KILL THE COPS NOW, straightaway a hole is pierced into our heart as two police officers were assassinated seated in their police car, accomplished by a man who openly stated to shocked by standers, "watch me do this, they kill one of ours we'll kill two of them".

All the while Mayor De Blasio at a press conference talks politics, and a need to come together never once explaining how he was going to accomplish this or how a person such as Al Sharpton is still walking the streets of New York, nor have we yet heard from Obama, or America's top cop Eric Holder. It would seem Al Sharpton remains to be their advisor. This man should be charged with inciting a riot and enflaming a dangerous situation, held in jail on a multi-million dollar cash only bond. I believe Al Sharpton is a community organizer just as Obama is a menace and remains so today, this is merely the results of their ideological relationship for dividing our nation, thus as he Obama, stated back in 2008 " to fundamentally transform the United States of America", as cohorts attempt to achieve this cohesive goal consolidating their efforts.

Thus we find these men Obama, Holder, Sharpton, De Blasio socialist all, cognitive of one another's goals and ought be in front and center for the joint effort.

I again find it important at this time to ask where in our Constitution lies the concept, impression, or suggestion of "protest marches" exist. Certainly it's not the first

126

amendment, as it reads, *"the right of the people to peaceably assemble, and to petition the government for a redress of grievances"*. May I once more submit to you, laying down one's body across the road to the Brooklyn Bridge, halting traffic is not peaceable assemble, neither is stopping traffic in Times Square to the hinderance of others. Furthermore, protesting by obstructing traffic walking down a main boulevard is in fact a misdemeanor and should have been brought to an end, immediately prohibited and those involved arrested.

The deaths of Michael Brown and Eric Garner were the perfect events for the experienced "Saul Alinsky style community organizers", exploiting these activities for use to incite, therefore affecting a market for and about their agenda. This criminal alliance is dedicated to the destruction of civil order and the rule of law within the cities of America. Notwithstanding, I remain optimistic there may still be time to defeat the tide of evil facing our republic, if our society turns to God and executes His precepts and put into action the visions of our founders. There may still be time, however the moment has cast its authoritative spirit upon us, a beneficial assignment of action and we by necessity, are required to move quickly in order to halt the flood of evil proceedings which draws closer each day. For me the feeling to set in motion the necessary measures is quickly parting, leaving me without the words to properly express the urgency for which the task ahead requires.

God will not fail in His promise to guide and support, Numbers 13 verses 31, 32, the Israelites failed to trust God in their oncoming battle, they believed victory was impossible, failing to remember God does not operate from a human prospective, a promise from God is a sure thing. Are we willing to stand against the pressures of popular opinion and follow His perceptions? Nevertheless it requires we begin to move, as a vehicle cannot turn directions unless it's moving, we are obliged to be in motion to receive God's assistance and trying to obey His design for our society. However I'm concerned the clergy arrives on the scene a bit weak, reluctant to lead the people due to the infamous law instigated by President Johnson some sixty years ago, 501(c) 3. This law suggest that clergy and the church shall not indulge *"in no part of the net earnings of which familiarizes to the benefit of any private shareholder or individual, no substantial part of the activities of which is carrying on propaganda, or otherwise attempting, to influence legislation (except as otherwise provided in subsection (h)), and which does not participate in, or intervene in (including the publishing or distributing of statements), any political campaign on behalf of (or in opposition to) any candidate for public office", (sub-section H has little or no relationship to this issue).* The leaders of Christian churches and groups have an obligation to have this law rescinded, or give it no consideration whatsoever. If there is to be any change in our republic's direction it's the clergy that ought to spearhead the change and be the impetus, the precursor generating the necessary enthusiasm, causing their church people to admire and respect them. I do believe if this were to happen many people would be converted, Christians along with a number of whom are on the verge, will justifiably edge away from our flawed secular politicians. The perception any change will come about due to any reasoning, for the so called conservative party "GOP" now having the control in the Senate, is merely a dream. I consider both parties are all about themselves with little if any concern for their constituents, the citizens that hired and positioned them to represent them along with others in Washington D.C. When one looks at the ideology of these two parties we find the Democrats saying their goal is to help working and poor folks through free food, housing, health care and even cell phones,

My name for these programs is "handouts", while there are some requiring help, most are simply lazy deadbeats, unwilling to work and have never understood the basic inner demand for work. It is without any doubt where our clergy has failed profoundly and fundamentally, therefore ultimately leaving a vacuum which government was more than delighted to fill, with your money, called taxes.

Republicans on the other hand have chosen to be all things to all people, passing on their agenda with nothing but empty words. I regard their willingness to return to God's ideals, pure propaganda for our republic and that sorry rhetoric not found in our founders, simply pure rhetoric, devoid of any significance. Furthermore, they propose doing more with less by cutting waste and corruption in government, now this is where I have attempted humor, doing this with many reservations and with numerous conditions, if anything they are the essence of squander, waste and corruption,

128

furthermore warriors attempting to increase our ideals through force rather than example. The truth is both parties have aspirations of large government thus having more control over our lives.

The Congress being in control of the budget, are now more than ever capable plus responsible and should decide what's necessary to be spent on obligations needed to operate the government, as defined in "Article One sec. eight", of course the politicians have long destroyed the provisions therein, for the needs of national governmental operations and failed creating projects best designed and controlled by the states, when managed correctly, our taxes would decrease dramatically. This sequence is but a dream, from the very beginning the founders proposed and intended a two party system, the idea being to debate different points of view coming from various areas of the union. Now they only argue for the exclusive purpose of gaining power, influence and money from we the citizens, taxes, it's quite difficult to ascertain and judge which party to place our trust, when both are corrupt, they are both habitually non- compliant with the Constitution, all their jabbering by no means distinguishing one from another.

At this point with respect to the illegal protesting, generally the Afro-Americans are missing the premise of our legal system, one could clearly see while in their haste to judgment, people such as Al Sharpton have deceived them for his own personal gain and future. Little expertise, rather a hatred of what they perceive to be fact, that white people have perpetrated this act upon them, while this may be true in a few cases, as their own people have sworn to a grand jury quite the opposite picture. Nevertheless, they believe this grants them the opportunity to vent which is a good thing, but when exercised properly. These people are driven by the media and agitators much like the Jesse Jackson and Ben Jealous, Black panthers, among others. Then we have Al Sharpton in a category by himself and one of his own making, nothing more than a low life criminal, moreover failing to pay his federal taxes, to the tune of one and half million dollars.

This attitude shows once again that distrust of law enforcement presents a grave danger to the civic fabric of the United States. I deem the responsibility of our elected officals is to clear the air of mistrust, since it is they which are the ones who caused this complex issue to occur in the first place. A police force is a Constituted body of persons empowered by the state to enforce the law, protect person, property and keep a tight rein on civil disorder. I am reasonably confident few of our citizens comprehend or appreciate the meaning of the Fifth Amendment, therefore missing the point of this essential and fundamental provision, totally lacking this knowledge. This dilemma clearly creates a problematic situation, to whom do we owe our allegiance, the protesters that seem ignorant of the law, the police or the grand jury and most of all the agitators, which include president Obama.

My reading of the Fifth Amendment seems to define, beyond a doubt, as part of the first clause, "unless on a presentment or indictment of a grand jury", this seems to embrace all questions with regards to the issue at hand. Now what troubles myself since president Obama and Eric Holder are both lawyers, why did they persist in being agitators and openly defending the protestors.

In defense of my past words being too strong, read this written by an Afro- American woman; in two separate videos uploaded to YouTube Monday, this unnamed woman posting under the username "Honestly Speaking" unleashed a tirade against Al Sharpton, calling him a "disgusting disgrace to humanity" and decrying the civil rights leader as a "race-baiting, tired, pathetic … no good for nobody a**." The woman started her fiery rebuke with a 50-second clip railing against Sharpton's recent revelation that he received death threats in the wake of the murders of NYPD Officers Rafael Ramos and Wenjian Liu.

*"Leave it to Reverend Al Sharpton to make two cops having been murdered about him. Nobody cares that you received death threats. Nobody cares about you. You are the reason this is happening," she proclaimed. "Take your old, stale, trouble-making, race-baiting, tired, pathetic, perverted, coke-sniffing no good for nobody a** go somewhere and sit down."*

As for De Blasio, she delivered a similar message. "De Blasio, Mike Brown is not your son.

*"You have been brainwashed into believing in a super duper space daddy or mommy, by bronze age goat herders". Your religion is not even original, your savior, is based on another so called messiah who existed centuries before yours came into being. Like I said, keep venerating your genocidal, child murdering deity, ignorance is bliss, and you are a most happy fellow".*

This attack along with many others against Christianity and even Catholicism globally, including the United States, is becoming stronger, while devoid of or little resistance from Christians and their leaders. I firmly believe as a nation we are becoming more and more secular and yielding a significant amount of faith in government rather than faith in God, the God our founders were so infected with, trusting God for strength and wisdom. This present hour demands resuming the specifics our political leaders and our churches along with the clergy, restoring the extremely basic ideals which founded this republic, without which we are doomed. While some speak of a wall between religious activities and government, I find in the

First Amendment that "government must refrain from establishing a religion, or prohibiting the free exercise thereof". Their fear and concern came from the past, British imposing their demands in this regard. However if a **wall** exist, it in no way ever suggest religious pursuits to intervene in governments affairs in any way, be restricted.

Another issue which occurs while referring to the attack on Christianity, is the issue of free speech. It appears the attack on both these subjects stem from our First Amendment, as both of these ideals work hand in hand and the persons writing them placed them at the top of their agenda. This provides for me, the importance they assigned to the two questions we are speaking of and their laying them out in words of very plain English.

While I may give the impression that all is lost, on the other hand, while it's true we are on the brink of disaster there is still time for change, as we have been provided a power from God and are willing to go down a course of profoundly new but difficult choices. Since our society has elected an uncomplicated route the results have left us in a situation with inadequate options, thus we ought to move ahead and improve our choices, we should act upon challenges that may create setbacks and problems for individuals and our society, there are essential and loftier goals to aspire, as God is our source of power.

The first item, maintain and be insistent, we need to be tough on our politicians to reduce, coordinate and/or orchestrate the many bureaucratic departments, then disband the Federal Reserve, go back to the Constitution. Then remove our illegal tax code and in the process the I.R.S. would survive no longer, therefore relish in its departure, as the billions saved would go to worthwhile issues and perhaps lower taxes. In what way may I ask, have citizens taken into account that for 125 years our national government stood and progressed without "income tax", our Constitution clearly defines the obligation which they are expressly duty-bound to subsidize? During those years all these obligations were fulfilled, the Congress never gave the people an impression of a great need for large additional funds being considered necessary. Nevertheless, in 1913 Congress explained a need for a small tax on large business and industry, this tax to be laid on their income from "whatever source derived and without apportionment among the several states"… This sounds to me an indirect tax which was already in existence, as the Supreme Court stated "no new tax had been written since the Congress already had the power to lay and collect taxes". For me it's the confusion in which the wording presents some questions, such as the word income. Examining Noah Webster dictionary we see his definition, "that gain which proceeds from, business, property etc. and/or applied to the gain of private persons". In Ballantine's law dictionary we find, for tax purpose the gain derived from capital, labor or both combined. Again in Noah Webster dictionary the word most often used, gain, is defined as "profit, increase or interest, to obtain by industry or the employment of capital, to get as profit".

Nevertheless, perhaps it's more appropriate letting me answer, thus explaining the main reason why again our Supreme Court perverted our Constitution and lied to the American people. Within our Constitution at Article One, sec.8 the limited powers to tax are enumerated for the national government, all else are reserved rights to the

132

states. This, for what reason or purpose is there to enumerate if a general power, could eclipse them. These are the rights bestowed to the states and enumerated in our Constitution. Let us remember, the union of the states was to *"form a more perfect union"* between one another. However, they would never ever give up their sovereignty, as each and every state had its own Constitution and government.

The Supreme Court invalidated state laws by prohibiting or restrictions, which lacks any basis in the text, since logic, structure or orginal understanding of the Constitution, must prevail. . In *U.S. vs Butler 1936* an earlier Roberts, wrote, *"the tax invades the reserved rights of the states. Therefore a matter beyond the powers delegated to the federal government, the tax is but a means to an unconstitutional end".*

This misuse of words which fall completely within the Affordable Care Act, where John Roberts stunned and annihilated many Americans reversing the word penalty into tax. When checking, I never found these words synonyms or an alternative word to be used for alternative expression, never.

The essence of my point stands on the fact the average American citizen works and is paid in exchange for his labor, where is the gain derived, there is no gain, no increase or profit, only an exchange of earnings for labor, the earnings being equal to labor. Once more our government deceived the American people, this was sold on the idea the general public as a whole would not be taxed. Trying not to get into the weeds too far, the reason government used indirect taxation rather than direct, as direct taxes would be utterly obvious and in all probability rejected.

The idea that more taxes are needed to properly meet the needs of a growing republic are necessary and are addressed in *Article one sec. 2, third clause.* However to this day that tax, a direct tax controlled and laid upon the individual soveriegn states, has never been approached as it's so simple the national government has not been capable to envision a way for cheating, or swindling the public. This tax is applied to each state individually according to its respective population, and Representatives. Therefore each state is obliged to collect the necessary funds from the citizen by whatever means the citizens select.

This is exactly why our Founders gave notice to King George of England, "taxation without representation won't get it". So a rebellious group of upstarts began a war only believing God would support their efforts. Read Patrick Henry's speech at the Virginia colonies delegation, called the ": give me liberty or give me death".

Why do we *pay income tax, ignorance,* when our early congress knew that in time there would be a need for additional funds, to support the efforts of the national principal body and provided for it in Article one, section 2, clause 3, read it for yourself.

So once again government crept and inched the idea forward of one percent at a time and until WW2 came the payroll tax (actually still income tax) to support the war effort, who could use rates that have risen and fallen over the last seventy years. This depending upon the idiocy of the people we hired to represent our interest. The cost to support their programs, which unelected bureaucrats are hired to administer and manipulate, are some triggers which caused taxes to escalate, the obvious alternative from here was regulations and more regulation, till the national government deeply broaden their control rather than the state governments, spelled out in the Ninth and Tenth Amendments.

As a matter of procedure, they have forwarded more or less some portion of the taxes they stole to the states, is primarily in a temporal sense if the states followed their guide lines. Our republic sadly became inoperative after we surrendered our original concepts and principles and worst have forgotten the God of our founders and the ideology He laid down for us to fulfill, His promise of "certain unalienable rights". Still applicable is the mark of character to the idea we need to pledge to each other our lives, our fortunes and our sacred honor, in other words find unity and self- respect along with self- reliance. Driving toward that goal will diminish the will and size of government, which should be our goal. In my life time, rarely have I seen government perform well, at its best, mediocrity, rather in all probability totally inept.

We are now in the midst of an election for President and we have at least twelve candidates, most if now all are unworthy to gain that position, nevertheless one will. The Republicans continue to suggest the necessity to ward off socialism, how crazy a statement, don't they realize socialism has already arrived. We have one a professed socialist, stating without question his beliefs and the designs of a socialistic system is the salvation for our nation. His corresponding individual says she isn't, rather her actions speak louder than words and she may be correct as I believe her to be a gangster. Therefore, should she like any other criminal be locked up, away from society in general, thus longer could she organize or systemize a scheme to cheat, steal and deceive the American public. This woman Hillary Clinton, has been a part of politics for more than thirty five years, she was our last Sect. of State. Her tenure in that office was a major disaster, cheated at every aspect then lied pertaining to criminal deeds.

The Republicans are fighting each other like dogs, spending the better part of their time crafting pathways to destroy each other. Arranging narratives of time past, saying we may be on the road to socialism, we're no longer on the road to socialism, we're on a launching pad to fascism, let's **come to our senses.** Why are Christians so complacent, if we pray only, do we really believe God will intervene, even so have Christians truly become repentant, let alone this republic come to their knees, reflecting upon both groups and taking into consideration all the factors, pondering seems to work for them both. One finds the Bible's positions in Isaiah, 53 – 6, *all we like sheep have gone astray, we have turned everyone to his own way, but the Lord hath laid upon him the sins of us all.* I'm sure you realize a theologian I am not, nevertheless while the reference is to our sins and Christ's redemption for them, I do believe it fits my objective, as it's sin which keeps us so far from the realization of the calamity we face.

Honestly, is one able to observe one individual capable to lead this nation, a nation in chaos and fundamentally starved for God, there are no tricks, President Obama had all the tricks. He so stated, he would fundamentally transform the United States of America, and he did so. Again we hear how necessary it's become to stop him and his ideology, stop him, he has already achieved his goal. It seems most persons consider he thinks differently than the majority of Americans and he will come around, what fools we are, **he is a Muslim. Are** we unwilling to see his allegance for them.

He has no use for our Constitution, his father and step-father were Muslim, as a young man he went to Muslim schools. Though he failed but tried to write a book about his father called "Dreams from my father" with his advance of 150,000.00 which he spent half with his wife in Tahiti and was forced to return the other half to the publisher. The book Dreams, was written by Bill Ayers with notes of events from Obama, to sort things out as best he could at the time.

The citizens of our republic are infested with beyond 70 various agencies and departments led and staffed by unelected personnel, I will present only a few of these agencies as examples, I have found you could locate a full list at Wikipedia. The National Asian Pacific center on aging, Office of the Federal coordinator, Alaska Natural gas transportation projects, Commission on key National indicators, Prevention of Genocide Task Force and which I found extremely hilarious, Center for Regulatory Effectiveness, as we are now swimming in regulations, an impediment in any attempt in growing our economy.

While all these ludicrous and outrageous agencies directions with insurmountable outcomes, a very distressing event happening today is the national government shoving cattlemen off BLM property, after years of their feeding on these grounds, improving them and under contract, keeping the water moving and under control, saving a significant amount of this land.

Here in New Mexico a war between county and forest officals exist. The essence of the dispute is over water the U.S. fish and wild life dept. concerning the endangered "meadow jumping mouse". My question, what about the endangered humans relying on the land and why do they assume some right to land they "stole" in the first place, within the sovereign state of New Mexico? Here a group of lackeys, quasi agency trying to muscle the cattlemen off the land used for years, struggling to appear as heroes for some mouse, the mouse may well be fine and probably will outlive most of us and I surmise the meadow jumping mouse has any knowledge of their heroes.

I find anyone examining how easily these departments are able to press their agendas, at an extreme cost to all citizens. If the cost which are passed on to we the people were instead removed from that department's own budget, this would reduce the number of deceptive and spurious charges brought against our citizens.

There seems a never ending supply of either corruption, stupidity, in fighting or right out derilection of duty, pluck your cream of the crop and the remains are an origin created incremental from nothing and far more than enough to pass around. Will Rogers identified them in this manner "when they joke it becomes law and when they pass laws they are a joke", this clearly is a well categorized account of our position, as a case in point this interval, this phase in our republic's future. As for Hillary and her never-ending past, problems. "As far as I am aware, no other Cabinet secretary in history was ever called for the release of his or her emails in their entirety and throughout his or her tenure," said Rep. Elijah Cummings of Maryland, who noted that last year the State Department provided 55,000 pages of documents and last month submitted 800 pages of emails from her own server, to the committee related to Benghazi. Although this materialized after Hillary left the post two years earlier, how can one be certain of honesty, not by her past activities? Guilt by her association with herself.

Benghazi may well be for the "anointed Hillary" her losing the crown, meeting her Waterloo as all her personal and political problems mount, and her inability to wisely dispense of them, shows her lack of skillfulness to keep under her control the negative events being exposed. The use of a personal email server, an encrypted server no less and in her home, where no one including the state department, all remained lacking any access to her files. This action on her part is a violation on its face, a breach and defiance of the Freedom of information Act, *5U.S.C.A.sec.552 also 5 U.S.C.552, PL, 104-231, 110 STAT 3048.*

Furthermore, the State Dept. has not displayed a form "OF 109"which must be signed by all State Department persons, including the Sect. herself, nor will Hillary confirm she had. Either way she should face criminal action. While we're at this juncture, the server was reduced by the e- mails her attorneys alone decided were personal. That idea sure makes sense to most of us!

Title 5 *Sec. 552.001. POLICY; CONSTRUCTION;*

*(A)*

*under the fundamental philosophy of the American constitutional form of representative government that adheres to the principle that government is the servant and not the master of the people, it is the policy of this state that each person is entitled, unless otherwise expressly provided by law, at all times to complete information about the affairs of government and the official acts of public officials and employees. The people, in delegating authority, do not give their public servants the right to decide what is good for the people to know and what is not good for them to know. The people insist on remaining informed so that they may retain control over the instruments they have created. The provisions of this chapter shall be liberally construed to implement this policy.*

*a This chapter shall be liberally construed in favor of granting a request for information.*

*Added by Acts 1993, 73rd Leg., ch. 268, Sec. 1, eff. Sept. 1, 1993.*

I believe this abuse of power and delusional thinking in reference to her authority is explained by her willful disrespect for the law. Thus her assessment of the Freedom of information Act requirement, *to provide access to public records includes not only a legal right of access, but a reasonable opportunity to avail oneself to the same.* The failure to provide and kept in hiding particular information and doing so I believe is criminal. We shall see if an examination of her activities brings this incident to daylight or if some manipulative proceedings spring her out, as in the past at least a dozen investigations were squashed acts regarding the Clintons behavior, especially with the Chinese. I for one, remember in particular where records were lost which the investigators needed, but two years after the investigation ended were found in an upstairs bedroom desk. So much for the Clinton regime and their never ending saga, plus their own rules of the road, laws which need never be related toward them.

A larger-than-life epic, an event our military trained the Iraq army at a cost of hundreds of millions of dollars, plus placing our people in harms-way. However at this time they and some Iranian military are fighting at Tikrit. This is a lost situation, since our effort no matter who wins we lose, on and on our cowardly President

138

digresses. One could go forward but you get the point, our republic has never been in greater danger. However, the Iranians and Iraqis turned tail and run.

I realize the dangers confronting our nation today and as I have stated before, we must return to our God given principles, the God of our fathers and the Constitution with God's help they could recreate our society and will again be blessed. Then follow the Constitution, word for word plus the principles and meaning from which it was written, in the era it was written. Hire people to represent our needs, fire the corrupt, liars and bandits in office, there are many and revolt if necessary, not unlike our leaders some 240 years ago. They fought for far less government control than exist today, they wanting to be free, choice was given by God. Government wishes to steal it away. *The separate and equal station to which the laws of nature and of nature's God entitle them. Unalienable rights are given by God, plus among others, Life, Liberty and the pursuit of happiness...Thomas Jefferson*

Now the State Department officials have said, "she may have violated federal requirements that official correspondence be retained as part of the agency's record", thus the beginning of an investigation by the F.B.I. and the office of the Attorney General.

President Obama stated he was unaware of this until receiving it from the media. Perhaps he forgot to mention this requirement to his first Secretary of State, remember he too is a liar.

Question, How many of government emails were in Mrs. Clinton's account without our knowledge, not clear, and neither is the process her advisers used to determine which were related to her work with the State Department and which if any were not, rather she determined before turning them over, for me this ambush was a big witticism on the American public.

The House Select Committee on Benghazi established by Speaker Boehner follows the evidence and collects facts. Last month, Chairman Trey Gowdy (R-SC) announced he would be interviewing 20 current members and former Obama administration officials, including Hillary Clinton, but only after receiving *all* of her relevant documents, including notes and emails.

"The idea the Benghazi Committee was unable to discover these previously unknowns, and before today unreported information, speaks for the need aimed at this committee. As a fact, while the Committee does not hastely move into every single discovery they reach, in my judgment simply speaks to their commitment. In particular people as Mr. Pompeo, Mr. Jordan and Mr. Gowdy I believe have conducted, a fair and impartial judgment of the facts found. *"Our interest here is not in producing a story, our interest here is in gaining access to all of the documents, all of the emails and all of the witnesses, therefore producing a final definitive accounting and one that is frankly worthy of the sacrifice of our four fellow Americans and worthy of the respect of our fellow citizens."*

In her confirmation testimony back in 2009, Hillary Rodham Clinton said: "We must use what I have called "**smart power**," the full range of tools at our disposal, diplomatic, economic, military, political, legal and cultural. Picking the right tool or combination of tools for each situation. With smart power, diplomacy will be the vanguard of our foreign policy."

The fact remains, flying millions of miles of travel, at our expense is not work, she came upon and shmozed with many Potentates, for lack of a better title, which in turn created many opportunities for contributing to the Clinton Foundation. Another fact, all the data in her account was not available to the citizens of our republic, the law covering this is called *"Freedom of information Act". 5 U.S.C. sect. 552. As Amended by Public Law No. 104-231, 110 Stat. 3048*

I am sure you remember the reset button with Russia, joke or sham, or both who knows her four years as Sect. of State was a joke.

On Wednesday, the House committee investigating the attack on the U.S. consulate in Benghazi, was forced to subpoena Clinton's communications regarding Libya and notified Internet companies that they have a legal obligation to preserve relevant documents.

During that time frame, emails to and from Clinton then went to servers in Colorado and North Carolina operated by the cybersecurity firm McAfee. That means at least some of her emails can be accessed by congressional investigators through McAfee's servers.

At a Capitol Hill news conference Tuesday, past House Speaker John A. Boehner (R. Ohio) called on Clinton to turn over her private e-mail server to a neutral third party to decide which of her e-mails should be public record. "I think this is the fairest way to make sure that we have all the facts that belong to the public," Boehner said.

Clinton said at news conference last week that she did not conduct any classified business using the Clintonemail.com address, but that she used it for both business and personal communications. Her office handed over about 30,000 e-mails last year when the State Department asked all former secretaries for copies of any and all communications they had.

Clinton said at a news conference the e-mails she turned over were work-related, and her office has said that most were between Clinton and State Department employees, they stated those whose work related emails used standard government e-mail addresses. Clinton said last week that she had deleted roughly half the cache, or about 30,000 e-mails, that she deemed personal. Hillary is a liar and 80% of Americans deem her an untrustworthy person.

With the FBI and State Department inspector general now investigating **Hillary Clinton**'s use of a private email server, her reputation for honesty is in the cellar, television networks were clamoring Sunday for reaction from the South Carolina congressman who chairs the House Select Committee on Benghazi.

*"Fox News Sunday" host Chris Wallace asked for Gowdy's reaction after playing a short clip of Clinton lambasting Republicans for playing "the same old partisan games" by politicizing her email scandal.* Gowdy replied that the investigation into Clinton's activities could hardly be defined as partisan, they were initiated by the Obama administration's FBI and inspectors general. And Clinton's own handling of the matter, particularly how she presented the involvement of longtime confidant Sidney Blumenthal, did her no favors, Gowdy said by his statement *"I get that she's*

*frustrated, her poll numbers are tanking". Folks who never thought about getting into the race are getting in the race. But she need not blame House Republicans for having her own personal server, for exclusively using private email for telling us the Sidney Blumenthal emails were unsolicited and then we later find out that they were not, after telling us there was no classified information, then we later find out that there was."* Gowdy remarked *"that when people are angry, they tend to react in one of two ways: They'll either look in the mirror engaging in self-reflection, or they'll lash out and blame outside forces, like non-existent right-wing conspiracies. Apparently, she's chosen to do the latter,"* Gowdy said.

The difference between Clinton and the others is they didn't exclusively use their personal email for government business, rather they significantly used the provided government email system as it was better protected. Subsequently, the fact is **no one** have their own personal server in their home for a period of time. Then she moved it at several intervals at least, to new locations.

18 U.S. Code § 2071 - Concealment, removal, or mutilation generally

*(a)      Whoever willfully and unlawfully conceals, removes, mutilates, obliterates, or destroys, or attempts to do so, or, with intent to do so takes and carries away any record, proceeding, map, book, paper, document, or other thing, filed or deposited with any clerk or officer of any court of the United States, or in any public office, or with any judicial or public officer of the United States, shall be fined under this title or imprisoned not more than three years, or both.*

*(b)      Whoever, having the custody of any such record, proceeding, map, book, document, paper, or other thing, willfully and unlawfully conceals, removes, mutilates, obliterates, falsifies, or destroys the same, shall be fined under this title or imprisoned not more than three years, or both; and shall forfeit his office and be disqualified from holding any office under the United States. As used in this subsection, the term "office" does not include the office held by any person as a retired officer of the Armed Forces of the United States.*

Which of the above unlawful activities may well be appropriate for Hilary Clinton actions? First willfully and unlawfully concealment, then removed and or obliterated, or destroyed, without creating a long list, thus the fact for the utmost part, both of the paragraphs apply.

Despite everything, her gall and past abilities to present deliberately and ambiguous or misleading positions, seems she is pressing forward, though she did express regret and apologized about the server. I believe she is sorry she was caught. However she maintained she had her attorneys check for private and government e-mails separating them and then turned over all government work.

Hillary has escaped immoral and criminal activities for more than thirty five years, let's hope this time the FBI will have the determination and sufficient resolute attitude to place her in prison for as long as possible, as she is a burden and detriment to society and our republic... rather than the White House the Big House. I believe it's my duty, and obligation to once more address Hillary Clinton's tenure as Sect. of State and what I have ascertain being the truth concerning her proceedings. Simply two occurrences involving her and Billy boy Clinton, being in the same given area at the same time. Top fundraiser opts out of Hillary campaign as Clinton Foundation hit by 'slush fund' verdict which compares it to the Al Sharpton charity. The Clinton Foundation CEO Maura Pally said "Yes, we made mistakes such as funds mistakenly combined, government grants and some other donations". Now to me that seems quite definitive, a sharp and clearly transparent explanation.


The Foundation faces criticism after reporting it received millions from executive who sold the uranium company to Russia in a State Department-approved deal, Pally said Canadian law prevented its partner from disclosing the donation. The foundation took in $140 million in 2013 and spent another $84.6 million on payroll operations and just $9 million on direct aid. All during this interval Billy boy was receiving 500 thousand to 750 thousand for speeches.


While the crux of her life brought a lack of spiritually, leading to destitution and a really sad pathetic life. Nonetheless, God requires I pray for her, asking for change in her life and a turn toward Him, seeking a path toward finding a need for transformation.

I do believe she has placed herself in a very deep-rooted situation and this time I'm afraid there is no one else for her to blame. It seems quite certain she will be charged. During that time, she enjoyed a security clearance identical to that of the President, the Secretary of Defense, the director of the CIA and others, it is the highest level of clearance the government makes available.

She had a classified clearance so that she could do her job, which involved knowing and working with military, diplomatic and sensitive national security secrets. The government guards those secrets by requiring high-ranking government officials to keep the documents and emails that reflect them, in a secure government-approved venue and to return any retained records when leaving office.

I have not seen Clinton's signature on any documents, but standard government procedure is for her to have signed an agreement under oath when she began her work at the State Department requiring her to safeguard classified records, and another agreement under oath when she ended her work plus that she had returned all records to the government.

She breached and disregarded both agreements, and she has violated numerous federal laws. As I write these words I find it sad, nevertheless I am only uttering the results of what she conspired against her own government. Strange how one contrives against oneself, as she spent an entire life to serve as president, in the course of her attempt she destroyed all endeavors and shattered all reason for such activities. Following are some of the crimes the Justice Dept. and the FBI in all, possibility accuse Hillary of committing: *First, 18 U.S. Code § 1924 - Unauthorized removal and retention of classified documents or material.*

**18 U.S. § 1924.**

**Unauthorized removal and retention of classified documents or material**

*(a)      Whoever, being an officer, employee, contractor, or consultant of the United States, and, by virtue of his office, employment, position, or contract, becomes possessed of documents or materials containing classified information of the United*

*States, knowingly removes such documents or materials without authority and with the intent to retain such documents or materials at an unauthorized location shall be fined under this title or imprisoned for not more than one year, or both.*

**(b)** For purposes of this section, the provision <u>of documents and materials to the Congress</u> shall not constitute an offense under subsection (a).

**(c)** *In this section, the term "classified information of the United States" means information originated, owned, or possessed by the United States Government concerning the national defense or foreign relations of the United States that has been determined pursuant to law or Executive order to require protection against unauthorized disclosure in the interests of national security.*

<u>Second,</u> Search 18 U.S.C. § 1519 : US Code - Section 1519: Destruction, alteration, or falsification of records in Federal investigations and bankruptcy

*Whoever knowingly alters, destroys, mutilates, conceals, covers up, falsifies, or makes a false entry in any record, document, or tangible object with the intent to impede, obstruct, or influence The investigation or proper administration of any matter within the jurisdiction of any department or agency of the United States or any case filed under title 11, or in relation to or contemplation of any such matter or case, shall be fined under this title, imprisoned not more than 20 years, or both.*

*U.S. code 18, part II, 205, 3101 - 18 U.S.C. § 3001 : Procedure governed by rules; scope, purpose and effect; definition of terms; local rules; forms - (Rule) - See more at: U.S. code18, II part, 20, 3101*

**Search 18 U.S.C. 1519, § 3101:, US Code - Section 3101: Effect of rules of court - (Rule) - See more at:** *U.S. Code18 part 11, 205, 3101*

A person at a town hall meeting asked Hillary, why she used her own e-mail and server. Hillary answered, "due to its being more convenient". Once more asked, "I thought it was illegal to use your own server, the subsequent idea proceeding its use, occurs when it could be misused and perhaps hacked". Again she said, "they have been throwing things at me for years and yet have failed to make any of it stick".

Please remain good-natured and follow my findings with regards to the probability of criminal activities on the part of Hillary Clinton. The law I'm suggesting is: *18*

*U.S.C.A. sec. 793* the 2003 Espionage Act, is very long and I will only impart the sections I believe she has violated, plus closed her eyes to and/or failed to disclose. I'm not a lawyer and may have inadequately presented the charges, if so you be the judge. For myself they seem quite simple and obvious.

The Espionage Act of 1917 & 918 was eventually superseded by a less onerous Espionage Act passed after World War II. However, remnants of the act, particularly the non-controversial parts, continue to exist in American law as of 2003 (e.g. 18 U.S.C.A. § 793). Below are sections D, E and F

*(d)*
*Whoever, lawfully having possession of, access to, control over, or being entrusted with any document, writing, code book, signal book, sketch, photograph, photographic negative, blueprint, plan, map, model, instrument, appliance, or note relating to the national defense, or information relating to the national defense which information the possessor has reason to believe could be used to the injury of the United States or to the advantage of any foreign nation, willfully communicates, delivers, transmits or causes to be communicated, delivered, or transmitted or attempts to communicate, deliver, transmit or cause to be communicated, delivered or transmitted the same to any person not entitled to receive it, or willfully retains the same and fails to deliver it on demand to the officer or employee of the United States entitled to receive it; or*

*(e)*
*Whoever having unauthorized possession of, access to, or control over any document, writing, code book, signal book, sketch, photograph, photographic negative, blueprint, plan, map, model, instrument, appliance, or note relating to the national defense, or information relating to the national defense which information the possessor has reason to believe could be used to the injury of the United States or to the advantage of any foreign nation, willfully communicates, delivers, transmits or causes to be communicated, delivered, or transmitted, or attempts to communicate, deliver, transmit or cause to be communicated, delivered, or transmitted the same to any person not entitled to receive it, or willfully retains the same and fails to deliver it to the officer or employee of the United States entitled to receive it; or*

*(f)*
*Whoever, being entrusted with or having lawful possession or control of any document, writing, code book, signal book, sketch, photograph, photographic negative, blueprint, plan, map, model, instrument, appliance, note, or information, relating to the national defense, (1) through gross negligence permits the same to be removed from its proper place of custody or delivered to anyone in violation of his trust, or to be lost, stolen, abstracted, or destroyed, or (2) having knowledge that the*

146

*same has been illegally removed from its proper place of custody or delivered to anyone in violation of its trust, or lost, or stolen, abstracted, or destroyed, and fails to make prompt report of such loss, theft, abstraction, or destruction to his superior officer—*
*Shall be fined under this title or imprisoned not more than ten years, or both.*

However, believing my case against Hillary has been fully presented, thus we will begin to move on, believing this is enough of Hillary with her arrogant attitude and expression of subsisting as superior, leading an unchallengeable life. ***What a fool we mortals be.***

One could go on and on, rather you have individually survived my inflicting you with my point by point explanation. The fact is we are not only facing the three persons I have selected, rather we are a divided nation, pitting liberal against conservative, Democrat against Republican. There is a profound divide, actually inordinate loathing, we are one people, how have we become so far away from each other. Now our republic is in deep rebellion, a dilemma here at home, even in an election why are members of the same party attempting to destroy one another. I am certain only with our God's help, the same God which created this once noble nation and granted us undeniable Rights and to assume the powers of the earth, the separate and equal station to which the laws of nature and of nature's God entitles them and are endowed by their Creator those certain unalienable Rights, among them Life, Liberty and the pursuit of happiness.

I challenge all who have listened to my dissertation to confront all politicians, vocally and/or with every means possible. It is only We the People who are able to negate secular, social corruption and immorality and political lawlessness in all three branches of the national government. Political persons involved in giving away funds of all kinds to folks, which only defeats the incentive to work. This intention is not for those unable to support themselves and needing help, while church's commitment needs to achieve far greater objectives, as they are obligated. As a result leaving a minute role on behalf of government, in most situations local governments do much better. So we must turn to God, again I repeat, the God of our framers, the Christian God, the one and only Almighty God. We are in need of Christian leaders who will stand up and lead, through prayer and whatever obligations demands us and because of inescapably action we shall reestablish Godly principles and take command of our republic. Then all else will spill into place, as this will effectively bring back our republic from whence it started, as a Christian nation.

With God's help we shall be able to turn our republic into the republic our founders battled and died, spending their fortunes to create a republic where we are the governing and chose from within who will serve our people, as we are free to do what we desire, that is freedom, which with God's help are the intrinsic means, ideas, from the people, never ever government. Thus making America again the greatest nation on the face of the world, morally governing from within, by God's grace controlling our economy and its militarily, asking God's Blessing for all our endeavors, then will our republic regain "that light upon a hill".

I beseech every so called Christian to face this dilemma, rather as a people finding ourselves mired in complex absurdities, useless excuses and whining, praying that somewhere, somehow along the way God will step up and bail us out. It's us who by necessity, must grasp hold from the multiple explanations. It is the need of every single Christian to become bold enough to press our derelict leaders and precisely with utmost accuracy leading our republic's path toward the once great Christian nation of the past. While Pastor Abedini sits in prison for his faith in our God, we sit on our hands or comfortably in church praying God to do something. It has come to pass, realizing what fools we dubbed "Christians" have become. A call is obligatory by our pastors for taking action, my brother's *conquering action*, as praying is the most fundamental, however engagement on our part must follow, as God has proposed, kill all these barbarian savages. Translated "guerrilla terrorist".

My meager ability to place into words the urgency confronting us face to face, the heartfelt and authentic words are better articulated by one Patrick Henry, these are but a few of his provoking and captivating declarations:

*Shall we gather strength by irresolution and inaction? Shall we acquire the means of effectual resistance by lying supinely on our backs and hugging the delusive phantom of hope, until our enemies shall have bound us hand and foot? Sir, we are not weak if we make a proper use of those means which the God of nature hath placed in our power. Besides, sir, we shall not fight our battles alone. There is a just God who presides over the destinies of nations... The battle, sir, is not to the strong alone; it is to the vigilant, the active, the brave. If we were base enough to desire it, it is now too late to retire from the contest. There is no retreat but in submission and slavery! Our chains are forged! Their clanking may be heard on the plains of Boston! The war is inevitable--and let it come! I repeat it, sir, let it come..... Gentlemen may cry, Peace, Peace-- but there is no peace. The war is actually begun! The next gale that sweeps from the north will bring to our ears the clash of resounding arms! Our brethren are already in the field! Why stand we here idle? What is it that gentlemen wish? What would they have? Is life so dear, or peace so sweet, as to be purchased at the price of chains and slavery? Forbid it, Almighty God! I know not what course others may take; but as for me,* give Me Liberty or give Me Death".

We may hear from Christian ministers to pray and as Pastor Dr. Jeffress stated he believed in praying first, then go kill them all and I believe likewise. This initiative was purposed by God in First Samuel chapter fifteen, verses one through five. The main conception of this passage was, *to destroy all things, including men, women, children, infants, livestock and all belongings.*

Now some will pervert this by suggesting this was in Old Testaments times. Most Bibles in their explanation and importance state: *They were an enemy of the Hebrews people and were guerilla terrorist.* This statement coming from scores of Theological Bible Professors.

If one deems the above incorrect, then the created and blessed Republic, which God created and fashioned, plus man deemed necessary to fight, giving their life, fortunes and honor, was all worthless and meaningless gestures.

If this appears pointed at evangelical Christians, gospel trusting plus, in Jesus Christ crucified and risen sitting on the right hand of God Almighty interceding for ME and you, it's for these motivations and senses, that it is true and factual.

All Americans need to behest God to uphold their repentant efforts and forgive their negligent conduct, there is no other manner, this is the only solution to our multilayered and numerous troubles. It seems to me quite apparent as there is little else but God, for us to appeal for help, as a republic, as a society and personally. We look to those trying to convince us they have the answer, if they advocate doing so without God, **they are liars**.

Returning to the Revolutionary era is our answer, they trusted God and believed He would support and attend their needs, today God is able and will if we believe, He is waiting for our change of heart and accepting His Son Jesus Christ, our only savior.

Please forget looking to government for help, simply looking at their record of corruption will show how inadequate and cowardice action with an appallingly miniscule sum of their performance has improved, and if as an example, a result through evidence would be the central indication leading the way.

Considering this trend, should bring into view their depths of fruitless actions and their inadequate vision for the future of our republic. Don't look to any man, accordingly any group of men as they will surely fail you, look for wise men who's strength, energy and goals, comes from God.

While I intended to close within a few more words, when a loss, truly notable and heart-rending occasion for both our Republic and the U. S. Supreme Court, Justice Antonin Scalia passed away. He in my opinion is unquestionably of immense stature and a demonstrative Christian man, goes far beyond his tenure in the Supreme Court. I am for want of grasping Gods special devotion, giving to our nation a man such as this, yet bringing the challenge of replacing such a person, seems quite impossible.

Seeking out any man of this prominent distinction in our history and for attaining a person so dedicated or true to the ideals of our republic requires the prayers of Christian people.

As he urged fellow intellectuals to be "fools for Christ" and once used an interview to underscore his belief in the *existence of the Devil*, and whose latest maneuver were, as he said, "*is for getting people not to believe in him or in God*".

These people fail to understand marriage, Antonin Scalia says it's no surprise that the

Supreme Court doesn't agree with the majority of the people on same-sex marriage. In fact, he was particularly snide not just with the decision that the majority made, but the manner in which it was expressed.

*"The majority opinion is couched in a style that is as pretentious as its content is egotistic,"* Scalia thundered in his dissent.

I again discover myself trying to unearth a man, who after the diabolical reign of the dictator President Lincoln. Finding the stature of Justice Scalia, one is obliged to fall back revisiting, Washington, Adams, Henry, Madison and Jefferson along with others of that era. Today the cast is quite barren, lonely of men with such integrity and the strength of character.

For a second time my concern over same sex marriage, answering in response: Scalia found this Kennedy line *"the nature of marriage is that, through its enduring bond, two persons together can find other freedoms, such as expression, intimacy, and spirituality"* Justice Scalia "distasteful".

*"Really? Who ever thought that intimacy and spirituality [whatever that means] were freedoms? And if intimacy is, one would think Freedom of Intimacy is abridged rather than expanded by marriage. Ask any experienced individual, expression, sure enough is a freedom, but anyone in a long-lasting marriage will attest that a happy state constricts, rather than expands, what one can prudently say."*

Another Scalia gem, exposed and made known in his view, *" that weddings and funerals were beyond doubt a place, but especially funerals, are the principal occasions left in modern America when you can preach the Good News not just to the faithful, but to those who have never really heard it."* I believe Antonin Scalia, perhaps unknowingly, though little passed him if anything, was a great leader of Christianity.

This is written not as an eulogy, rather an exemplification of a man, the loss of which our republic has sorrowfully experienced and must shoulder, replacing him is probably imposible, nevertheless we must prayerfully move forward and shall find someone who will carry the Court forward in a positive manner and may God bless the Scalia family.

The Republican Party appears to be in the midst of an abnormal departure from common sense, a divergence over the candidacy for President of our republic. A man, Donald. Trump seems devoid of any or perhaps little of what this office requires, or demands of him.  As we have just spent seven and one half years with a man who's vast experience, was as a community organizer. Many found him a great orator, convincing countless voters he was their man, rather all the while he warned he intended to fundamentally transform the United States of America, as he inflicted us with his narratives.  While his agenda was an unholy, obsessive perception, leading us on the road to socialism, whereas the people were all too willing to accept his on the job training, not once but twice, how foolish we remained.
Now we are considering a man who is without a clue, as how the execution of our Republican form of ruling functions, his bullying attitude and behavior expose the obvious methods he employs.

As with Hillary Clinton it's a coronation, either she will be queen or he will become king, forgetting their need to work with Congress and the courts plus our Constitution. His dialogue is generally repetitious and bombastic, with little substance.  God forbid any of his or her opportunities, to appoint perhaps several possible appointments to the U.S. Supreme Court.

Then we have three men destroying each other, neither willing to become a patriot giving virtuously and beneficially their support to the other, therefore to the benefit of the Republic. Their egos will crush their intentions, Sad, sad, sad, such is their actions or lack thereof, their egos guaranteeing them failure coming to pass, pure and simple self-centeredness.

I suppose generally all elections are concerning one's ego, he or she believes they know what's best for a nation, organization or group etc. and are able to lead them best. Meanwhile I think it appropriate conveying information regarding these two

152

candidates in particular. I am certain the issue would be highly realistic and feasible to scrutinize Hillary Clinton and Donald Trump as Presidential candidates quite a bit closer. Doing so justly, examining while seeking the truth with regards to their character, therefore finding a reason to choose or not, ne Where or what aligns or is in conjunction with these activities, lays our President. Shall it be fraud, deception perversion? The protection of the two-witness rule of the Constitution in such case extends at least to all acts of the defendant which are used to draw incriminating inferences that aid and comfort have been given. P. 325 U. S. 33. In a prosecution upon an indictment charging treason by adhering to enemies of the United States, giving them aid and comfort, in violation of § 1 of the Criminal Code two of the overt acts alleged and relied on were: P. 325 U. S. 34.neither one as candidate for President of our Republic.

Shall we begin with Hillary Clinton, as she was Secretary of State, flying around the globe transacting ideas and business viewpoints with foreign nations, I might add not very successfully. Although she was able to setup speeches for husband Billy boy, as much as 750,000.00 dollars, not bad. Billy's response was "he needed to pay the bills", ever the clone of a politician.

Then there was Benghazi, the tragedy of our Ambassador's death along with three other patriots, caused by the negligence of Hillary Clinton. However, after lied, stating it was due to a movie negative to Islam, while it was indeed a planned raid by terrorist. Why was Hillary & Obama flanked by the flag-draped coffins at Andrews Air Force base, of four Americans murdered as a result of their incompetence?

This from a past military man; *Thank you. I'm a vet and this crap disgusts me. Fast and Furious, and now the WH is blatantly supporting Al Quaida? How many royal decrees? Treasonous dogs, all of them. Our pussy Congress needs to arrest and imprison then hold public trials and public executions for these seditious domestic enemies of the United States of America. Hillary needs to be held accountable for her MANY previous murders. Bill, Samantha Power, Susan Rice, etc. It's time to clean house. That swamp draining needs to happen, and all the Democrat traitors need to pay for their crimes. It's sickening how many of them are murderers and rapists; maybe that's why they get along with the Mohammedi's*

I chose inserting this statement as it represented my feelings, only said more skillfully and competently with considerable feeling, here are a few others; *I talk to my son in Afghanistan & despair for America as our leaders sacrifice our sons & daughters on the altars of their political careers and personal enrichment. The American surrender of territory to the Taliban has begun, and jihadists are coming out of the caves and over the border for their last chances at killing Americans before they retreat to the U.S. The alphabet media, once the Constitution-protecting Fourth Estate, is now the freedom-destroying homeland-hating Fifth Column. It's hard not to be depressed if you are aware of the forces aligned against America, inside and outside our borders, and see the feckless waste-to-God-and-country politicians' betrayal.* Your son is a far better person than Mrs. Clinton ever could be. Please thank him for his service. Yet another individual; *I believe history will judge these two as the lowest of those in American politics.*

There is a Judge who may well judge them and immeasurably harsher than history could so, with forever conceivable potency. And the punishment being far worse

as there is a God who is observing us all.

Returning to Hillary, we find her failing to sign a simple single page form required all person in the State department, plus having her own e-mail account, using it for State work. Now it's found to have been used by Hillary Clinton sending or receiving emails from her top aides warning about dangerous security conditions. Furthermore, it's discovered her e-mails originate on her own server and holding highly critical information. After this discovery, her server was moved and her denial began, till this today. Nevertheless, the FBI and the State found the server after having been moved the second time.

Now, whereas we know information from the Justice dept. and the FBI, had been sending confidential information and other information of extra top secret national significance which of course needed to be held repressed and concealed by all and any possible means from our enemies.

Meanwhile the above documents soon to be sent to the federal grand jury determining her future. As this action by Hillary Clinton having used her personal e-mail and her email server to send this extremely confidential information was deprived of proper government available protection. Hillary's server sat in three hidden and different locations, unprotected and foremost concerning this matter she LIED, she lied repeatedly and persistently about all these factors. Then again this is not something of a new nature for Mrs. Clinton.

**WASHINGTON, Jan. 26 1996** Hillary Rodham Clinton testified for more than four hours today before a Federal grand jury investigating whether there has been obstruction of justice at the White House in the inquiry into the First Lady's former Arkansas law firm. With a nervous but determined smile, Mrs. Clinton emerged from the extensive grand jury session and declared, "I tried to be as helpful as I could in their investigation efforts." The transcripts the Grand Jury was pursuing, happened to be found little more than two years later, in her bedroom desk.

Twenty years later with significant political misadventures in between we still find Hillary in trouble. ***Joseph E. diGenova***, *a D.C. lawyer, said he believes that two FBI investigations were underway on political corruption, one of which involved the presidential candidate. Based on reports agents are asking questions about the foundation, "it seems to me it is the subject of a second prong of the investigation."* From the Daily Caller;…

*Clinton "should be terrified of the fact that he's (Mr. Pagliano) been granted immunity. Now, what does granted immunity mean? Only a federal judge can grant immunity. A federal judge will only grant immunity if a sitting jury is ready to hear testimony from the immunized person. So we know a couple of things. We know the recommendation we were waiting for from the FBI to the Justice Department has already made its way from the FBI to the Justice Department."*

*"We know FBI agents and Justice Department prosecutors are working in tandem,"* Napolitano added. *"We know that they went through this lengthy process of interviewing Mr. Pagliano and finding out what he knows and deciding it's so valuable they need him to say it to a grand jury and the only way he can say it to a grand jury is if they promise not prosecute him and hence he gets immunity and we also know they're going to seek indictment because they would not be immunizing him and thereby inducing him to spill his guts, unless they wanted to indict someone. And we don't know who it is. There's four or five people in between Pagliano and Hillary Clinton."*

I have previously given material evidence with regards to Hillary Clinton's behavior, together with her arrogance and audacity. So much for that candidate.

Moving on to the bombastic blowhard Donald Trump, where should one launch and establish his position. Personally, I've ascertained his personality, finding it nothing short of a bully, not unlike a child when he's unsuccessful in receiving what he desires. He said many times "if anyone take a pass at me I will swing back much harder" and so he maintains this posture at his rallies and the debates, consequently his character and demeanor would remain the same as President. As an example today 3/16/'16, he the don, has refused to attend the scheduled debate for 3/21/'16 and said he thinks the candidates have had "enough debates," and he plans to make a speech that night instead.

In addition to his bullying, lying, quite observable criminal activities, outrageous statements and general misbehavior, now his cowardly comportment is apparent. After his comment that he would not debate, Kasich's campaign said the Ohio governor had hoped to face off against Trump, and the campaign indicated that Kasich would only attend if Trump does, "If [Trump] changes his mind, we will be there.". Trump's past performances have shown how weak his knowledge of our Constitution, foreign affairs and dealing with our enemies, stating he would murder the families of the terrorist, only works to exposes his lack of awareness for international agreements and places us at their low level, but that is his mind set. This cowardly wimp wants to be the President of our Republic? I was under the assumption the Republican National Committee made that decision as it's for the peoples benefit.

Furthermore, in an interview on CNN, the Republican presidential frontrunner said that *he does not regret never asking God for forgiveness, partially because he says "he doesn't have much to apologize for, I have a great relationship with God. I have great relationship with the Evangelicals". "I am not sure I have, ever asked God for forgiveness, I don't feel God needs to get involved".*
This is the same man who late last year, when interviewed by Frank Luntz, *"that when he has done something wrong, he tries to correct his error without getting God involved".* God said *"Be still and Know that I am GOD! I will be honored by every nation in the world" Psalm 46,10 "Cast your cares on the LORD and he will sustain you; he will never let the righteous fall"* (Psalm 55:22).

I do believe, all of us are in need of forgiveness, not once but many times a day, in the Old Testament we find, Proverbs 24:16 (ASV). Though a righteous man falls seven times, and rises up again; but the wicked are overthrown by calamity.

"A civil racketeering lawsuit against Donald Trump can proceed as a class action lawsuit, a federal judge has ruled, in a major incremental victory for a former student accusing him of running a bogus investment university.

The ruling by Judge Gonzalo Curiel means that a California businessman named Art Cohen can sue Donald Trump on behalf of anybody who bought seminars from Trump University after January 2007. The lawsuit accuses Donald Trump and his university of violating federal racketeering law by scheming to defraud students into paying thousands of dollars for useless real estate investing classes.

Recent clashes at Trump rallies have created havoc in St. Louis, Chicago, Cleveland and elsewhere, some other candidates have spoken out on this issue. After unrest at Donald Trump rallies over the weekend, Luntz says anger surrounding his campaign is only getting worse. He joined CBSN to talk about the 2016 race and the concern over violence at Trump rallies.

Texas Sen. Ted Cruz, who is chasing Trump in the fight for delegates, told NBC's *Meet the Press* on Sunday that it's wrong for protesters to try and shut down Trump rallies, but "at the end of the day in any campaign, responsibility starts at the top. And it is not beneficial when you have a presidential candidate like Donald Trump telling his supporters, 'Punch that guy in the face.'" Ohio Gov. John Kasich, who faces a critical primary in his home state Tuesday, blasted Trump on Saturday for creating "a toxic environment" that "has allowed his supporters, and those who sometimes seek confrontation, to come together in violence."

Florida Sen. Marco Rubio, who also desperately needs a win at home this week, said Sunday the businessman exploits Americans' anger and anxieties. "There are people out there that listen to this stuff and we don't know how they're going to react," Rubio said on ABC's *This Week*. "And he keeps putting this stuff out there. We're going to have an ugly scene here; we already have seen these ugly scenes."

Kasich and Rubio each raised doubts over the weekend over whether they would back Trump in the general election should he win the nomination.

It is my opinion, due to the average American animation and their distressed feelings with the government in general, they are more than ready for change, any change. Their excitement is similar to the 1930s when Germany along with all Europe plus the United States were in a state of depression. The citizenary were thoroughly stressed and distressed more than ready for an answer to their dilemma. People afflicted by misfortune seek leadership and seldom the best. However, whom ever has the quickest no matter how adverse the remedy for the immediate problem will prevail. In my view Trump will set these people aflame, as this is his goal.

The conventional analysis of the economic situation in Germany in the 1920-30s was of tremendous hardships and were experienced both locally and for the nation as a whole. These hardships followed from ordinary post-war (First World War) conditions and also from the harsh reparations and other punishments exacted on Germany by the victorious Alliance. While this conventional view has been challenged, it is precisely the view that Hitler and the Nazi Party adopted in their rise to power in the 1930s.

158

The conditions were very favorable to the Nazi Party and, as such, is considered to be an important event in German history. Exposure in Hugenberg's widely read newspapers gave the Nazis free publicity and party leader Adolf Hitler became a household name in Germany– In addition to this, campaigning with the mainstream right-wing parties, gave Hitler a credibility he had lacked before. The dynamism and youthful enthusiasm of the Nazis, which had appealed to Hugenberg appealed to voters too. In December 1929, the Nazis gained 11% of the vote in Thuringia and made gains in other states.– In March 1930 the Reichstag ratified the Young Plan.

Certainly I'm comparing Donald Trump to Adolf Hitler and events in Germany and some of our Republic's parallel thinking, or lack thereof. However, by no means quite the same. Nevertheless Christianity is beset by obstacle and challenged by our own government, while little in this regard is questioned. I still cannot find, aside from a few true Christians, not yet significantly challenged by any so called Christians Rather I'm suggesting, Mr. Trump is by no means a man willing to deal, his own words plus a bully making demands like no other candidate. At one point insisting *"the party be nice to me or I will run as an independent"*. This man having no plans, no ideas and a poor if any understanding of our Constitution, is preying upon the existing situation of anger, stressed feelings, some beginning to reach a fever pitch due to inadequate action in Washington. Feeding on the exasperation and resentment of our citizens, failing to create anything other than problems, a leach proven many times over, this is the character of the individual Donald Trump, merely a bully.

However this man Donald Trump to me, turns up little better than Hillary and reminds me of Adolf Hitler, only instead he asserts he is really, really rich, which suggest to myself he has more money than Hitler could have dreamed.. Therefore, be careful as we may get more from Mr. Trump than we bargained to receive.

These expressions taking from the word of God "Knowing that tribulation produces perseverance; and perseverance, character; and character, hope" (Romans 5:3-4); " If we confess our sins, he is faithful and just to forgive us our sins and to cleanse us from all unrighteousness" These are the promises God has for returning our culture and republic to its original designs and initiatives. Nevertheless, in my opinion Hillary Clinton, Bernie Sanders or Donald Trump, all are cut from a similar cloth, thus unfit to serve our Republic in any position, let alone becoming our President.

The fact, we are facing quite a conundrum, nonetheless these are the circumstances and only a strong Christian movement, motivated with God's help through prayer, shall overcome the particulars we are encountering and praying for the intellectual capacity needed to face the necessary action on our part. At this pressing time to support any of the other candidates, rather than Hillary Clinton, Donald Trump or Bernie Sanders. **The** arrogance of Hillary while under a FBI investigation **is** beyond intelligent thinking or comprehension, causing me to become angry and beside myself. Sorry about my attitude but it scarcely seems possible in any respect.

Donald Trump is certainly further from reality, he has stated if he acquires eleven hundred delegates (1237 needed at least) and is not chosen candidate, "*there will be riots in the streets I'm telling you riots in the streets, all hell will break loose, like you never seen*".

These words coming from a man who wants to become President, I have never heard words like those except from communist Third World Countries. Following this wild utterance he told our Speaker of the House he had better be aware of his ideas and follow his viewpoints, or trouble will follow.

Let me continue with this thought for those considering Donald Trump for president, I am impressed with his attractiveness to the angry mass crowds, angry at the present GOP control of Congress in both the House and the Senate. In the prosecution of their duties have failed to keep their promises to We the People, nevertheless, Mr. Trump is not the person required for president of our Republic and I will try to present to those who may be thinking of him as so and why I suggest.to think otherwise.

Whereas while I am with the idea he may win the nomination, we must think of the general election, despite the fact that the Democrats continue bombarding him, this is the person they wish to face. The reason being, in all polls Mr. Trump vs Hillary

160

Clinton he's a loser. He may be correct in the idea he can raise a nightmare for the all the Congress persons, so what if he has lost the general election.

We find Ted Cruse leads Hillary Clinton by twenty one points (21) in an average of polls taken, isn't this our goal no matter the race for candidate. Another point, we have no idea how many Democrats voted for Trump in the primaries, regardless vote Democrat for Hillary in the general election. This is their goal, knowing the Republicans have many open primaries.

May I suggest this is what's happening, not a situation we can control other than to get behind Ted Cruse, one who can win this November. Another problem we had many candidates (17) and still have one who has no chance of getting 1237 still needing just under 1100, there aren't that many delegates remaining. One can't read his mind and it is his choice, still it would seem more patriotic for Mr. Kasick to remove himself from the fray, as Marco Rubio whom had more votes than he had accumulated until today.

This is to my mind a real and true assessment of the agenda facing our nation at a very crucial time. The idea of presenting these facts were not in my original thoughts, then the candidate situation arose over Hillary and Trump. These two individuals are by far the utmost corrupt individual persons we could be considering for president of our Republic. However a way should be found to stop this critical occurrence.
Hillary Clinton has federal law enforcement, state and federal courts plus Federal Judicial hearings, chasing after her for at least thirty years, right up to the present day. Her behavior all through these years has been nothing short of criminal.

Donald Trump is no less a wild individual than her, as he has stated, *"I know the people in congress and how corrupt they are, I've given millions, to both parties, I know how to deal. Then too I given donations to Hillary and the Democrat Party"*.
Let's not forget San Diego attorney who is representing Cohen, in seeking damages under the federal Racketeer Influenced and Corrupt Organizations Act. .Trump also will ask the judge in the case, Gonzalo P. Curiel, to recuse himself because of what his attorney called "animosity toward Mr. Trump and his views."

A wall the length of our border with Mexico and said "the Mexicans are going to pay for that wall", more exactly the President of Mexico laughed stating "that will never happen".

Then there are his ties with the mob, Trump's ties to New York and Philadelphia crime families go back decades and have been recounted in a book, newspapers and government records. "The mob connections of Donald are extraordinarily extensive," New York investigative journalist Wayne Barrett told CNN in an interview. Barrett, the author of the 1992 unauthorized biography "Trump: The Deals and the Downfall," wrote that Trump's life "intertwines with the underworld."

Again I have found Donald involved with Mr. Felix Sater a Trump business associate who pleaded guilty in a major mafia-linked stock fraud. Learning of Saters's activitives and knowing Sater's involvement and well aware of his background, nevertheless Trump became implicated with Sater's activities. Regardless hired him in a business development role, which included the title senior advisor to Trump, furthermore Sater had an office in the Trump Organization's Headquarters. Sater's criminal past initially drew attention because of his ties to Trump. Still today Mr. Trump believes he is fit to become president of our Republic, wow. While that sounds like the kind of great deal-making that Trump brags about, his business record and his economic proposals have come under intense scrutiny during his White House bid this year. From deporting millions of immigrants to inciting a trade war with other countries, Trump has made many grandiose promises over the course of his campaign. Most of his platform is based on improving the U.S. employment picture, but while he's focused on giving Americans a break thus creating job, rather his plans would cost the federal government trillions of dollars and many economists say they would be nearly impossible to carry out. Since 2012, the German bank has lent Mr. Trump more than $300 million through its private bank. Most recently, it committed to lending Mr. Trump $170 million to help with the ongoing renovation of the Old Post Office building in Washington, which the businessman is converting into a luxury hotel.

Again I sense he has the qualities of a Hitler style temperament, qualities which are part of his persona, *per-sona non grats,* a person to whom he or she is unable to represent for the country of their origin. His demeanor is similar to Adolf Hitler, due to wild statement and creating an atmosphere leading to the incitement of a crowd, therefore generating increased anger.

Listening to hear from the candidates about Social Security, I fail to be informed as to their ideas as how they are going to approach these massive problems facing us NOW

Since 2012, the German bank has lent Mr. Trump more than $300 million through its private bank. Most recently, it committed to lending Mr. Trump $170 million to help with the ongoing renovation of the Old Post Office building in Washington, which the businessman is converting into a luxury hotel.

Again I sense he has the qualities of a Hitler style temperament, qualities which are part of his persona, *per-sona non grats,* a person to whom he or she is unable to represent for the country of their origin. His demeanor is similar to Adolf Hitler, due to wild statement and creating an atmosphere leading to the incitement of a crowd, therefore generating increased anger.

Listening to hear from the candidates about Social Security, I fail to be informed as to their ideas as how they are going to approach these massive problems facing us NOW. It has been a "third rail issue" for several decades. Here we are and it's upon us with a vengeance devoid of any real solutions. Why are the candidates fearful to approach this very crucial subject currently facing our Republic.

Another serious issue lacking solutions is our national debt, determination of real concern is a question which must be resolved. These matters are issues we are waiting to be addressed by the candidates and why I have focused upon the needs previously brought to your attention plus other erupting subjects on current necessities.

I believe and am of the opinion the above information is sufficient for bring to thoughtful people some of the necessary facts to make a wiser decision.

There is without a doubt, any longer a reason for continuance of these congruent thoughts and comments, at least I hope that is so, therefore I will close and pray my words have been unencumbered and clear, therefore, as a result identify with others.

My sincere desire for God's blessing upon all who have patiently read my words, taking them to heart and my desire for their Godly Christians prayers for aspirations worthy of the republic God ordained.

Therefore continuing to plead for the profound love of God, that He may place a blessing on this Republic, praying our people, real Christians in particular will pray for forgiveness as both are in desperate necessity of His redeeming power.

I have written these comments, assertions and arguments humbly, praying God will use these simple words, though my study and reading with analysis. Nonetheless merely to inform or educate those caring and willing enough to hear these words, most if not all inspired by God, penned by a mere sinner, but saved by grace.